Building Positive Self-Concepts

THE BURGESS EDUCATIONAL PSYCHOLOGY SERIES FOR THE TEACHER
Consulting Editor: John F. Feldhusen, Purdue University

Building Positive Self-Concepts

Donald W. Felker

Purdue University

BURGESS PUBLISHING COMPANY • MINNEAPOLIS, MINNESOTA

To Evelyn
and our children

Copyright © 1974 by Burgess Publishing Company
Printed in the United States of America
Library of Congress Card Number 74-76647
SBN 8087-0620-9

3   4   5   6   7   8   9   0

Preface

The tutor was working with a fifth-grade boy in the remedial reading program by using a suffix wheel. She was trying to teach him the meaning of words ending in "less." The first word which appeared when the wheel was turned was careless. "What does that word mean, John?" "Well, that means *me*, because my teacher is always telling me how careless I am with my work." "Let's try another word." "What does this word mean?" as useless came upon the wheel. Without the little laugh, this time John said, "That's really *me*. My mom is always telling me how useless I am around the house." The teacher talked a bit about the meaning of useless and careless and said, "Ready? Here is another word. What does this word mean?" as worthless came upon the wheel. With no smile and with a deeply serious tone, the answer came back, "That's *me*, because I'm not worth a thing to anybody in this world!!"

This book is for people who work with children. People who have something to say and do which will help a child to feel worth something to someone in this world. All of you have met children who seem to have abilities and who seem to have many things about them which would make them feel good about themselves. Yet these children have learned to feel and think badly about themselves. If you have worked in a classroom, you know that these children are not likely to succeed in school and, even if they do succeed, they are not going to enjoy it. You also know from working with children that it is extremely difficult to help a child who does not like himself and that this type of child is a source of concern to most teachers. If a child dislikes himself, it clouds everything else he attempts to do and seems to thwart everything which you as a teacher try to do to help him.

In this book an attempt is made to give you knowledge which will help you in understanding and helping the child who has a negative view of himself and which will help you to keep children from developing a negative view of themselves as they meet the challenges of school life. For a child to gain self-esteem or to view himself in a positive way, it is necessary for him to feel that he "belongs," that he is "competent," and that he is "worthy." When a baby is born, he or she does not have any of these feelings, but he or she very quickly begins to develop them. The basic thrust of this book will be to tell you *how* the child develops or fails to develop this sense of belonging, competence, and worth. In this process of learning how to feel about himself, each individual comes into contact with significant persons who, to a large degree, will determine what view he is going to learn. As a teacher, you will be one of the persons who will significantly influence children in how they think and feel about themselves.

The outline of this book will follow children as they grow. It will begin with early infancy and look at the development of self-esteem through adolescence. At each of the stages of development (infancy, school age, adolescence), the things which significant persons can do to help the child develop a positive self-concept will be emphasized. The purpose of this book is not only to give you knowledge but to help you guide your behavior in such a way that you help children to succeed and enjoy it because they feel good about themselves.

September 1, 1973   Donald W. Felker

Contents

Chapter 1

Self-Concept Development
and Enhancement

John Quincy Adams held more important government offices than anyone else in the history of the United States. He served with distinction as President, Senator, Congressman, minister to major European powers, and participated in various capacities in the American Revolution, the War of 1812, and events leading to the Civil War. Yet at age 70 with much of this behind him, he could write, ". . . My whole life has been a succession of disappointments. I can scarcely recollect a single instance of success in anything that I ever undertook" (Kennedy, 1956).

What can explain such a difference in how a man looks at himself and feels about himself when compared to how others evaluate him? Such differences are difficult to explain, but experience testifies to the fact that they do exist. The teacher and every child with whom he comes into contact have areas of thought and feelings about themselves which are unique to them and different from the thoughts that other people have about them. Some people see themselves as being more competent than others see them, and some see themselves as less competent than others see them. Some people rate themselves as less likable than others do, and some rate themselves as more likable. The same is true of how individuals rate their physical appearance in comparison to how people around them rate it.

Notice that terms like "nicer than they really are" or "less competent than they really are" or "better looking than they really are" are not used. The question of what is "real" depends on the perceptions of individuals and can never be definitely determined.

Two questions will be considered in this chapter: What is self-concept? and, Why is it important?

What Is Self-Concept?

Self-concept is the sum total of the view which an individual has of himself. Self-concept is a unique set of perceptions, ideas, and attitudes which an individual has about himself. The view which an individual has of himself is unique and to varying degrees is different from the view that anyone else has about him. Remembering the aspect of uniqueness is helpful when dealing with children, because it forces the teacher to attempt to see things as the child sees them. One of the ingredients of good photographs of children is that the photographer catches the scene from the eye of the child. This may mean sitting on the floor looking at adult kneecaps, or lying on his back looking at stomachs that stick out and hide faces, or simply crawling and seeing nothing but the hands moving in front of him. Leontine Young (1966) in the book *Life Among the Giants* has attempted to catch the feeling of what it is like to be a small child in a large adult world. Adults can never really feel as the child feels or see things the way he sees them, but adults can learn by trying.

While each individual's view of the world is unique, it has more shared parts than the view which individuals have when they look inward. Recently my wife said to our three-year-old boy, "You don't smell good" and received the quick reply, "Me not stink. Me not mess pants. Me too big boy!" The indignation, the feeling, and the perception were his. We can smile at it; we can understand the words. But the feelings and vision that the child had of himself at that moment were uniquely his.

The uniqueness of the view which individuals have of themselves is comprised of three main factors: perceptions, ideas, and attitudes.

Self-Perception. Smells, sounds, tastes, and tactual feelings all come from the surroundings, and individuals constantly receive and absorb sensory data. Much of the sensory data is about themselves, and, when it is about themselves, it is unique to the individuals.

Close your eyes and then quickly visualize a picture of yourself. Think about that picture. Did you see yourself as heavier than you are? Or did you see yourself as more slender than you are? Did you see yourself as you are or as you used to be? Every individual sees himself differently.

Every individual also has a unique auditory feedback. Can you remember the first time you heard your voice on a tape recorder? Did it sound like you? Probably not to you, but it did to other people. This is because you receive much of your auditory feedback from inside your mouth and throat, while other people hear what comes out. For example, I always hear myself as having a moderately pitched voice, but what comes out is a voice with a higher pitch. The impression that I have of my voice is unique because what I receive is not what other people hear and there is simply no way that others can share in what I hear.

In addition to having this uniqueness of perception, individuals often hear different words. Have you ever tried to moderate between two persons who are arguing, and have you had to say, "Wait a minute, he did not say what you said he said?" Usually, people do not purposely change what people say; they simply do not hear the same words the same way that they were said. A colleague of mine had a sign on his door that reads: "I know you believe you understand what you think I said but I'm not sure you realize that what you heard is not what I meant." Everyone receives sensory data in a unique way so that it is not "raw" data but data filtered and interpreted by the receiver.

The same is true of all sensory perceptions. No two people can experience the same smells, tastes, or tactual sensations. The experiences individuals have through the perceptions they receive provide the basis for the self-concept. These data are unique, and they are the basis of the ideas and attitudes which an individual has toward the self.

Self-Ideas. The self also contains a set of unique ideas, and ideas are the central factor in the term "self-concept." The set of ideas which people have about themselves defines who and what they are. It is only as they absorb the sensory data and attach meanings to it that they can be said to have a *self-concept.* The meanings attached to sensory data are the conclusions that people come to about themselves from perceptions of their environment. As meanings become definite ideas, they operate to define and in turn give meaning to new data which is received, and the whole process becomes circular. Nothing is received in a raw, uninterpreted way, and, at the same time, what is received is incorporated into the whole set of self-referent ideas or concepts which the individual has developed.

In the process of giving meaning and getting meaning out of the data received, we draw conclusions about ourselves and begin to see ourselves in abstract terms. If you were to make a list of words which you use in describing a child, you might come up with words such as dependable, intelligent, helpful, considerate, obedient, mischievous, etc. As you look at these words you find that they usually do not refer to any one specific behavior or incident. They are all words which we have developed to deal with abstract qualities. We do the same thing when we define ourselves. We use words such as good or bad, smart or dumb, lovely or ugly. All of these words express conclusions to which we have come from the data which we have received and gathered about self.

The child or adult who has characteristics which are considered undesirable by those around him is quite likely to develop a "conception" of himself as being undesirable. There is much research, for example, to indicate that children and adults both think that the individual who is overweight is undesirable. When given the opportunity, people assign all types of undesirable characteristics to the individual who is fat. They say that he is more likely than other people to be lonely, lazy, ugly, etc., and even that he is more likely to cheat, lie, and be stupid. It has been shown also that individuals who are fat tend to rate themselves as undesirable. The tendency of individuals who have characteristics rated as undesirable by others to begin to see themselves as undesirable raises particular problems for individuals who are physically unattractive, physically handicapped, or who come from minority groups (when there is prejudice against those groups). These persons may have a particularly difficult time developing a positive self-concept because of the continual bombardment of negative ideas from the environment.

Self-Attitudes. The third aspect of self-concept is that of self-attitudes. In addition to receiving perceptions and developing these into ideas about what kind of people individuals are, individuals develop a set of attitudes toward themselves. Perceptions are received and come to individuals from the environment. Ideas are developed from perceptions and are internal thoughts about the self. Ideas and internal thoughts develop into attitudes which are aimed at the self. Attitudes occupy the dual role of both having and receiving. People have attitudes, and they aim them at themselves.

The unique set of feelings which individuals have toward themselves comprise the self-attitudes aspect of self-concept. According to

Morse and Wingo (1969), "Attitudes are emotionally toned ideas directed toward or against something." From this definition it can be seen that most attitudes are of the subject-object type. An individual has an emotionally toned idea directed toward or against something and that something is external. For example, John loves Mary. John is the actor and Mary is the object of the emotion. Self-attitudes are unique in that they are inner-directed. The subject or the individual who feels and expresses the inner-directed attitude corresponds to the object or the individual against or toward whom the attitude is being directed.

Because self-attitudes are directed inward, the emotions aroused by these attitudes are particularly powerful. Everyone directs attitudes (emotionally toned ideas) toward others and, at the same time, perceives the attitudes of others toward them. External attitudes can be avoided if they are negative or painful. But negative self-attitudes cannot be avoided; how can one walk away from oneself? Like the cartoon of the man on vacation who says, "I thought I could get away from things by going on vacation but I find that I am still with me," individuals cannot escape their own negative self-attitudes.

However, children often must face negative attitudes from external sources which they cannot avoid. How does a child remove himself from parents or teachers who have negative attitudes toward him? He might get away for a short time, but so much of his life is under the control of others that he does not really have the option of removing himself from a home or a classroom where he feels negative attitudes directed toward him.

Another way in which individuals defend themselves against the negative attitudes of others is by rationalization. One of the most common rationalizations maintains that the negative attitude is unjustified and that it is an indication of fault with the person that holds it, rather than with the object of the attitude. I recently heard two young girls talking. One said, "I don't like your new coat." The other answered, "It's not my fault if you have poor taste." The question of who had the poor taste is debatable, but assigning undesirable characteristics to others rather than to oneself is common practice. It is more comfortable to think that someone else has poor taste than to think that oneself has poor taste. But what happens when the idea of having poor taste or the feeling of dislike because of poor taste is a self-directed attitude? One cannot blame the one who has the attitude, because one would still be blaming oneself.

Self-directed attitudes are more powerful because they are not easily controlled by the usual defenses individuals use to handle negative attitudes directed toward them. If an individual feels that someone dislikes him, he can choose to avoid them or to rationalize about why they are wrong or mixed up in their feelings. But he cannot avoid himself, and he cannot effectively escape the situation by saying that the person expressing the negative emotion is wrong.

The self-concept is an extremely powerful factor in the growth and development of human beings. Part of the power comes from its uniqueness. Every individual has a concept of himself that consists of a set of self-directed perceptions, ideas, and attitudes. Anyone who attempts to tell an individual that reality is different than what he sees, feels, and thinks is likely to have a difficult time convincing him. I remember once when I was a child and the school district had free dental care. All of the dental work was done with an anesthetic gas. Another fellow and I got into a fight in the schoolyard over an argument about what the gas made you see. I had a vivid and clear memory of seeing green snowflakes. I don't remember what he saw, but one of us contradicted the other, and then we began arguing about who was right. It ended in a fistfight. It was an argument that had no answer, and each of us is faced continually with the same thing. Feelings and perceptions are unique. It is interesting that I can still remember what I saw under the influence of the anesthetic gas but I cannot for the life of me remember what the other fellow saw. His perceptions did not have the force of my experiences. It is this uniqueness and force of one's own perceptions which contributes to the importance of the self-concept.

Importance of the Self-Concept

The self-concept is a dynamic circular force in human lives. Every human is vitally influenced by those around him. The people who are important to him influence what he thinks of himself. The experiences which an individual has every day indicate to him that he is competent or incompetent, good or bad, worthy or unworthy. As though he were an individual in the center of an arena, he receives information and attitudes from all sides at once. This information comes to him from the outside and influences what he thinks about himself. In other words, the self-concept is forged by the pressures exerted upon an individual from the outside. But the self-concept also is an active ingredient in an individual's experiences. Experiences mold and shape the self-concept, but the self-concept has an active, dynamic role in shaping experiences. This active influential process gives the self-concept its primary importance, particularly for those who are attempting to understand the behavior of children.

The self-concept is important because it determines an individual's actions in various situations. Not only is it influenced by what happens, it determines how an individual will behave in a wide range of situations. The role of the self-concept is threefold. The self-concept operates as a mechanism for maintaining inner consistency; the self-concept determines how experiences are interpreted; and the self-concept provides a set of expectancies. Each of these three factors is a powerful determiner of behavior.

Self-Concept as a Maintainer of Inner Consistency. A number of researchers in personality have dealt with the first factor—the idea that human beings operate in ways which will maintain an inner consistency. If individuals have ideas, feelings, or perceptions which are out of harmony or in opposition to one another, a psychologically uncomfortable situation is produced. This psychologically uncomfortable position has been labeled "dissonance" (Festinger, 1957). An important aspect of dissonance is that there is a strong motivation to be comfortable, and, if dissonance makes an individual feel uncomfortable, he is likely to take any sort of action that will remove this uncomfortable feeling and allow him to feel comfortable again.

One of the first writers to connect this type of reasoning with self-concept was Lecky (1951). It was Lecky's argument that an individual is a unified system with the problem of maintaining harmony between himself and his environment. In order to maintain this type of harmony (it is interesting that the opposite of harmony is dissonance), the individual may refuse to see things in the environment; he may refuse to accept as valid things which other people tell him about himself; or he may strive to change things about himself or others.

What an individual thinks about himself is a vital part of internal consistency. It is not so much that the uncomfortable feelings come because two things are actually different but that dissonance is caused when an individual sees two things as being different.

Therefore, the child or the adult will act in ways which he thinks are consistent with the way he sees himself. If he feels he cannot do a task and that he is dumb, then he is likely to act and behave in such a way as to come out looking dumb. A few years ago I was working with a boy who scored high on standardized intelligence tests. Both on group tests and on two individual intelligence testing occasions, he had come out with I.Q. scores in the 115-125 range. This would indicate that he had the ability to master tasks which require verbal and mathematical skills. It was puzzling that he was not doing well in English and mathematics at school. In a counseling session, the boy said that he could not do the work because he was "not smart enough." In the conversation, remarks were made about the fact that he was smart enough to do the work, and the standardized test scores were used as evidence that he had the ability to cope with the work. The next semester when the regular intelligence tests were given what scores did he obtain? You guessed it—his I.Q. score had dropped down to the 85-100 range. While many questions could be and have been raised about the validity of such tests, I was firmly convinced from my experiences with the boy that he *needed* to score low on the I.Q. tests so that an inner consistency could be achieved. Higher scores were inconsistent with his view of himself as being not smart enough. He had been told that he had done well on a test and that this showed that he was able to do the work, and a lack of harmony between his view and other evidence had been created. The resulting dissonance was so out of harmony with the view he held that the idea tended to make him uncomfortable, just as an orchestra playing dissonant chords causes listeners to become uncomfortable. The boy brought things back into harmony by doing poorly on the next I.Q. test he took. Then there was no lack of harmony! It is interesting that he did not change his view of himself but that he acted in a way consistent with that view. It was the view that determined his behavior, not the behavior that determined his view.

Human beings have a tendency to act in ways which are consistent with the view they have of themselves. This strong motivating force to bring actions and happenings into harmony with their self-view makes the self-concept powerful and important. Teachers have frequently said in workshops that they have had a child take a test, receive a low grade, and then reply to the teacher who had been trying to convince them that they were capable, "See, I told you I was dumb!" The unspoken part is probably, "and I have just proved it to you and to myself."

Self-Concept as an Interpretation of Experience. A second reason why the self-concept is a powerful determinant of behavior is that it shapes the way in which individual experiences interpret things that happen to us. Every experience is given a meaning by the individual. Exactly the same thing can happen to two people, but one will interpret it one way, and the second will interpret it another. If a young man offers to help three women across a busy street, one might interpret it as a kindly act; the second might interpret it as an insult about her age and ability; and the third might interpret it as an improper advance and call a policeman. Each of these interpretations is dramatically influenced by the view that the woman has of herself.

Just as there is a strong tendency to act in ways which will show that one's behavior and one's view of himself are consistent, there is a strong tendency to interpret experiences in ways which are consistent with individual views. This factor makes it extremely difficult to change a self-concept that is formed and operating. Teacher trainees are frequently asked what they would do with a child who has a negative self-concept but average abilities. The teacher trainees are asked to propose two *specific* behaviors and not suggestions such as "give him more attention." For instance, they must say what they would actually do to give the child more attention. These trainees almost universally come up with: (1) make him a committee chairman, or (2) look for more instances in which to give him verbal praise for some of his actions. It has been pointed out that these two are an indication of the American tendency to refer everything to a committee and the current obsession with behavioral praise techniques. While both of these approaches are good starting points, they have the same limitations as other actions—that is, there is no way that the teacher can be assured that the child is going to view these actions positively. If the child has a negative self-concept, he could interpret these actions negatively. He might think: "See, I told you I was dumb. If I were not, why would the teacher be telling me that I am not. Is she trying to convince herself?" Or, "Being as dumb as I am, why is she appointing me chairman of the committee? She must really have it in for me. She is trying to show me up in front of the whole class, so everyone will see how stupid I am." There is no action that a teacher can take that a child with a negative self-concept cannot interpret in a negative way. No matter how positively others might interpret the action or how positively the teacher might mean the action, the child can still interpret it in a negative way. This makes the self-concept and the forming of a positive self-view extremely important. The self-concept is like an inner filter—every perception that enters the individual must go through the filter. As each perception passes through the filter, it is given meaning, and the meaning given is determined largely by the view the individual has of himself. If it is a negative view, every experience is stamped with a frown. If it is a positive view, each new experience is stamped with a smile.

Self-Concept as a Set of Expectations. The self-concept operates to determine what individuals do in situations, and it operates to determine how individuals interpret what other persons do in situations. The third part of the self-concept's power and influence is that it also determines what individuals expect to happen. This set of expectancies has been identified by some researchers as the central facet of the self-concept. According to McCandless, the self-concept is "a set of expectancies, plus evaluations of the areas or behaviors with reference to which these expectancies are held" (McCandless, 1967). There is an old story about an Irishman who is so sure that a Scotsman is going to insult him that he becomes angry on his way to see the man. He keeps imagining all of the things that the other man is going to say to him and how he is going to answer. As his expectations of being insulted grow, his anger flares. Finally, he marches up to the man's door and, when it opens, punches the Scotsman in the face before anything is said by either person! The Irishman's expectancies, not any real insults, directed his behavior. He expected to be insulted and acted on that expectation.

Similarly, children who are anxious about school frequently say something like, "I just know I am going to make a fool of myself" or, "I just know that I am going to fail that test." While some of these statements are attempts to elicit encouragement, some of them reflect a set of real expectancies. The child views himself in a certain way, and this determines how he is going to develop his expectancies.

People who view themselves as worthless expect others to treat them in a manner consistent with this expectation. A third-grade boy who had been deserted by his mother on three occasions is a good example. On the last occasion the desertion was concurrent with his father's arrest on a felony charge. The boy and his brothers were taken to the county home where he was labeled by the older children as the "jailbird." After leaving the county home, he was placed in a relative's home where there was intense hatred for the boy's father and severe punishment of the children by their new father figure. The severe punishment was accompanied by statements like, "You are just like your father and, if you keep this up, you will end up in jail just like him." When he entered the third grade, the boy had been involved in two stealing incidents and a number of disruptive and malicious mischief activities. As part of the program for working with the boy, the teacher kept a folder of the boy's work. One of the things which became glaringly clear was that the boy saw himself as someone who was going to end up in jail. One of the boy's assignments had been to write a story about the astronauts. The boy pictured himself as an astronaut who made the first trip to the moon. He got out of the spaceship, stepped to the ground, and was immediately arrested and thrown into jail by the moon police. He had landed in a no-parking zone!

Although this is an extreme example of a self-fulfilling prophecy, every individual carries with him a similar set of expectancies which operate to determine how he is going to act. If he expects good experiences, he acts in ways which bring them about. If he expects bad experiences, he acts in ways which make these expectations come true and then says to himself, "See, I was right." Children who perceive themselves as being unlikable expect people not to like them and then either act in ways consistent with this or interpret everything so that it fits with this expectancy.

Recently, a teacher described a boy whom she had in her class. He had been shuffled from one first-grade class to another since none of the teachers could handle him, and he had made numerous trips to the principal's office for punishment. In addition he fought constantly with other children. Finally, the teacher took him from the classroom to a vacant room and said: "James, you make me so mad and frustrated that I could just quit teaching and leave the school today and never come back. Do you know why I feel that way?"

"No!"

"Because I want to help you and I don't know what to do. Do you think I want to help you?"

"No."

"Do you think I like you?"

"NO!"

"Do you think the other kids like you?"

"NO!"

"Well James, if I did not like you what could I do?"

"You could take me to the principal and get me expelled." (Expelled is a pretty big word for a first grader.)

"Well, that should prove to you that I do care about you."

The teacher went on to try to work out some actual behaviors which would help change James's feeling that he was not liked. Notice that James did not think that people liked him and so he acted in a way which would make people dislike him and in a way which showed that he expected them to dislike him.

Self-Concept and Other Characteristics

Self-concept exerts a powerful influence as a determinant of behavior to maintain self-consistency, as a determinant of the meanings individuals give to experiences, and as a determinant of what they expect. Recognizing these influences leads to the hypothesis that self-concept is related to other characteristics, and research has supported this hypothesis. Positive self-concept is related to other desirable characteristics, and negative self-concept is related to other undesirable characteristics.

The relationships between self-concept and achievement, anxiety, self-responsibility for success and failure, prejudice, and internal language seem particularly important. Although a vast number of relationships could be discussed, these few have been chosen because they are characteristics of importance to schools and people who are working with children. These relationships are also well documented, whereas many relationships in the area of self-concept are not well documented and reliable (Wylie, 1961). The brief review of these relationships will be limited to those aspects which should be of particular interest to teachers.

Self-Concept and Achievement. It is well established that a relationship between self-concept and academic achievement exists (Wylie, 1961; Purkey, 1970). It is consistently found that positive self-concept is related to good academic achievement. This positive relationship is found for early elementary pupils (Wattenburg & Clifford, 1964), intermediate elementary pupils (Williams & Cole, 1968), and high school pupils (Shaw & Alves, 1963). The relationship is found in both black and white populations and in groups with learning problems of a serious nature (Caplin, 1969; Gorlow, Butler, & Guthrie, 1963).

Consistent findings showing this relationship raise the question of what mechanisms are operating to produce the relationship. The individual with low ability who meets failure would be expected to develop a negative self-image. But the relationship between self-concept and achievement seems to be based on more than inadequate ability. It has been found that self-concept adds significantly to the prediction of performance even when ability measures are taken into account (Binder, Jones, & Strowig, 1970). It has been found that low self-concept is characterized by significant underachievement; that is, the individual with a low self-concept does less well than expected when only his ability measures are taken into account (Shaw & Alves, 1963). One explanation which can be given is that achievement and self-concept interact. The low self-concept could produce lower performance, which in turn would feed the low self-concept, which in turn would produce lower performance.

Another possible explanation for the relationship is that low self-concept inhibits the individual's participation in learning tasks. It has been found that high curiosity boys have higher self-concepts than a counter group of low-curiosity boys (Maw & Maw, 1970). Various aspects of creativity have also been found to be related to self-concept (Felker & Treffinger, 1971). If the curious and creative person is more able to seek out information and tasks, a low or negative self-concept could inhibit this behavior and produce lower performance.

There are two findings of particular interest to teachers. One is that the positive relationship between academic achievement and self-concept appears to be more definite in boys than in girls. Any study which finds this relationship in a sex-mixed group is likely to find it more significant in the male population than in the female sample (Roth & Puri, 1967; Sears, 1970). This finding is consistent with the majority of self-concept research findings in which self-concept relationships in boys appear to be more stable and predictable. It could also indicate that achievement is a more crucial self-concept factor in boys. It could be that girls have other areas in which they can receive positive feedback or that achievement is less a problem for girls, and therefore adequate achievement is almost a universal factor in the female samples.

The second finding of interest to teachers is that reading has been found to be a vital factor in relationship to self-concept. Self-concept is a better predictor of reading achievement than ability measures (Wattenburg & Clifford, 1964). The relationship exists through the elementary school years (Williams & Cole, 1968) and on into high school (Robeck, 1964). It is found for both boys and girls (Hebert, 1968). Considering the importance of reading in school performance, this relationship is not surprising. It does point out, however, the dramatic influence which words and word-related activities have on self-concept.

Self-Concept and Anxiety. The relationship between negative self-concept and high anxiety has been well established in populations that are widely different in both age and geographical area (Coopersmith, 1959; Cowen, et al., 1965; Durrett, 1965; Lipsitt, 1958; Mitchell, 1959; Pilisuk, 1963; Rosenburg, 1963; Stanwyck & Felker, 1971). It has been argued that this relationship may be based on the fact that some individuals are more open to expressing negative thoughts about themselves. Since an admission of anxiety is a negative aspect and low self-concept requires the admission of negative qualities, individuals who admit anxiety on one test are likely to admit it on the other. This reasoning requires the assumption that people who have high self-concepts are hiding or falsifying negative qualities. Since there is no relationship between a lie scale and self-concept, this reasoning seems a weak explanation (Stanwyck, 1972). The general relationship between high anxiety and low self-concept is confirmed even when the anxiety measure is a more specific measure. Test anxiety is related to self-concept in much the same manner as general anxiety (Lekarczyk & Hill, 1969; Sarason & Koenig, 1965). It has been found that specific situational anxiety is related to low self-concept (Felker, 1972). Apparently, anxiety is bound up in the mechanisms which maintain a negative or positive self-concept and influence the manner in which an individual will respond to situations, particularly those involving achievement or evaluation (Felker, 1972).

Self-Concept and Locus of Control. The concept of locus of control was developed primarily from the learning theory of Rotter (1954) and refers to the individual's perception of whether his successes and failures are under his control or whether some outside force is in control. If the individual thinks that his successes and failures are under his control, he is said to have high internal control. If he believes that his successes and failures are under the control of some outside force, he is said to have high external control.

In addition to being related to other personality variables (Lefcourt, 1966; Watson, 1967), locus of control has been found to be related to areas of direct concern to the schools (Crandall, Katkovsky, & Crandall, 1965; Dissinger, 1968). The individual's perception of his control is related both to performance in school (Messer, 1972) and his attitudes toward school. Flanders, Morrison, and Brode (1968) found that during a school year students with high external locus of control had greater change in the direction of negative attitudes toward school than students with high internal locus of control.

The relationship between self-concept and locus of control is complex. It could be predicted that self-concept would be positively related to internal locus of control on the basis that the individual who feels that control is outside of himself would feel helpless and powerless and hence have a low self-concept. In actual investigations with children, however, the relationship seems sex-related and related to the success factor. It was found with a fourth-grade sample that the self-concepts of boys had a negative relationship with internal responsibility for failure; that is, boys with high self-concepts tended to put the responsibility for failure on other persons. The self-concepts of girls, however, had a positive relationship with success; that is, girls with high self-concepts tended to put the responsibility for success on themselves. This would suggest that boys maintain a positive self-concept by denying responsibility for failures and that girls maintain a positive self-concept by taking responsibility for success (Felker & Thomas, 1971). These findings were confirmed in another study in which it was found that boys with high self-concepts tended to set high goals and that a significant portion of them then denied responsibility for failure if the goal was not reached (Kay, 1972).

Self-Concept and Body Build. An individual's physical appearance is another influence on self-concept. In general, it has been found that if an individual has either a body which is not favorably stereotyped by the society or a body which is erratic in its ability to accomplish tasks, self-concept is likely to be affected negatively. It has been found that handicapped children of different races tend to have more negative self-concepts than nonhandicapped children (Richardson & Emerson, 1970). Those children with the most visually obvious handicaps tend to have the most negative self-concepts, and this seems to be particularly devastating for girls (Meissner & Thoreson, 1967). There is also considerable evidence that deaf children usually have more difficulty developing and maintaining a positive self-concept (Craig, 1965).

The effects of physical handicaps on self-concept could be due partly to the decreased competence and efficiency of the handicapped child. But physical appearance, exclusive of competence, apparently influences self-concept. It has been argued that if an individual has a body appearance that has negative connotations in society, he is likely to learn from his social interactions that he should regard himself with the same negative connotations which society attaches to his physical appearance (McCandless, 1967; Staffieri, 1967).

The majority of investigations into physical appearance and self-concept have looked at the physical dimension of body type. It has been found that individuals can be reliably classified on three dimensions of body type: linearity, muscularity, and circularity. The technical terms for these three dimensions are ectomorphy, mesomorphy, and endomorphy (see McCandless, 1967, Chapter 9, for a good summary of these dimensions). It has been found consistently that the individual with the muscular body build receives positive ratings, the individual with the linear body receives some positive and some negative ratings, and the individual with the circular or rotund build receives negative ratings. Although some studies have shown that girls, in contrast to boys, regard the linear type as the most personally desirable (Caskey & Felker, 1971), both girls and boys rate the round type negatively (Caskey & Felker, 1971; Staffieri, 1967).

If the societal ratings extended only to physical characteristics, it would not be so damaging, but the negative ratings often extend to all types of moral and personal dimensions. In studies using children as subjects, most frequently the round individual is rated "dirty," "stupid," "mean," etc. (Staffieri, 1967; Caskey & Felker, 1971). It is also important that an individual's body build does not influence the type of ratings which he gives to body types. This means that individuals with a negatively rated body build often accept the ratings of society and rate themselves accordingly.

It has been found that both boys and girls have differences in self-concept which are related to body build (Caskey & Felker, 1971; Felker, 1968; Felker & Kay, 1971; Kay, Felker, & Varoz, 1972). The difference is predominantly due to the lower self-ratings of those with the round, fat, body build.

The relationship between body type and self-concept is important for teachers in two ways. One is that teachers are a part of society and tend to adopt the societal stereotypes, unless they make a conscious effort not to do so. First reactions to individuals are often determined by their visual characteristics. If the teacher has immediate negative reactions due to the body build of the child, the child starts at a disadvantage.

Secondly, individual children with undesirable body builds need help maintaining a positive self-image in the face of peer and adult derogation. Obesity is a self-concept problem, and the individual who has a round body type is facing the problem continually.

Self-Concept and Prejudice. The relationship of self-concept to prejudice deals with the large question of self-acceptance and its relationship to acceptance of others. Common sense might suggest that if an individual accepts himself and rates himself highly, this would lead him to reject others and to rate others lower. This reasoning is based on the idea that an individual has only so much acceptance, and, if he uses it all on himself, he does not have any left for others. But it is better to look at acceptance behavior as learned behavior. If the individual learns acceptance behaviors in one situation, it is likely that he will be able to exhibit the same type of behavior in similar situations. The individual who has learned acceptance behavior in relation to himself is more likely to generalize it to other individuals.

Hoffer (1951) has developed an armchair theory of prejudicial and excluding behavior in which self-derogation is the central dynamic force. It is Hoffer's idea that an individual who hates himself can only tolerate himself if he attaches himself to a group and then attributes all of the positive group characteristics to himself. Then he is allowed to "cover up" his negative self-feelings with good group feelings. Hoffer also contends that the degree of prejudice is determined by how broad the group is. If the group is very exclusive, it will entail a high degree of prejudice because it is necessary for the members to maintain that anyone who is outside the group is a negative person.

Although Hoffer's ideas may seem extreme, the basic contention that people who reject others generally have low self-esteem is important to the teacher, because any program of self-concept enhancement is carried on in the school social situation. The relationship between self-acceptance and acceptance of others suggests that such a program should deal not only with self-attitudes but also with attitudes toward others.

Self-Concept and Internal Language. Language is the central factor in the development of self-concept. It has been argued (McCandless, 1967) that the development of real language at the approximate age of 18 months to two years is the beginning of the self-concept. The term "concept" assumes the attachment of a name to something which encompasses a number of variables, some of which distinguish that thing from other things. The development of the self-concept entails the attachment of the term "self" or "me" to the set of characteristics that are "me" and distinguish "me" from other things and persons in the environment. The role of language is crucial in formulating this concept.

In addition to freeing individuals from specifics and allowing them to deal with things in abstract form, the role of language carries other important dimensions for the self-concept. Kohlberg, Yeager, and Hjertholm (1968) have pointed out that acquiring internal direction-giving is a developmental process which increases the individual's control over behavior. The process of giving self-rewards, including verbal self-rewards, has an effective influence on behavior.

Rewarding the self, particularly with verbal rewards, is related to self-concept. One explanation of the relationship is to regard the verbal labels and descriptions which the individual develops in forming the self-concept as a pool of statements which he uses to refer to himself. If these are negative statements and adjectives, he will say predominantly negative things to himself about himself. Marston (1965) has pointed out that this use of internal language may be one way of connecting internal self-concept with an external activity if the statements are vocalized. The relationship of positive self-language to self-concept has been investigated, and this approach has been found to give accurate predictions (Felker & Thomas, 1971). Statements which children choose as good to say to themselves have been found to be related to general self-concept (Felker & Stanwyck, 1971) and have been found to produce a stronger relationship than performance alone (Felker, 1972).

This relationship between self-reinforcement and self-concept is important for teachers because they deal so much with the language development of the child. Language development should include attention to the internal language which the child is using, particularly when it is being used to evaluate and reinforce or to reprimand. The fact that children learn "bad" as one of the first self-evaluative terms indicates that much of the social environment is designed to teach the child self-derogation rather than self-esteem (Rhine, Hill, & Wandruff, 1967).

Self-Concept Theories

In addition to those who have studied self-concept through research on empirical relationships, a number of other psychologists have attempted to look at self and self-concept from a theoretical point of view. These psychologists have used the idea of the self in explaining the mechanisms of behavior. It is not possible to discuss the ideas of these theorists in detail in this book, but a brief historical overview of the development of self-concept theory will be helpful in understanding the current state of self-concept research and ideas.

The beginning of the study of the self-concept in the United States owes much to William James and Sigmund Freud. William James was a philosopher-psychologist who considered the ego to be the individual's sense of identity (James, 1890). Identity had various aspects including the mental, spiritual, and social. Perhaps the importance of James is that he considered the perceptions which an individual had of himself an important variable in understanding human behavior. He remarked once that whenever two people meet there are really six people present. There is each man as he is, each man as the other sees him, and each man as he sees himself. According to James this view which each has of himself includes feelings and perceptions about self which are distinct from or different from reality but it is equally important for understanding.

Sigmund Freud's work and writings added the vital dimension of "dynamics" to the ideas of the self. While Freud's lifetime overlapped that of James, they seem to have had little in common in their approaches. Freud's work was primarily an outgrowth of work with persons suffering from hysteria, i.e., persons who had suffered the loss of some physical function without any apparent cause.

Freud developed a complex theory which rested heavily on the role of the unconscious in motivating and determining human behavior. As Freud revised and enlarged his theory, the concept of the ego took an important place. The role of the ego was to organize and moderate between the natural forces of the id and the cultural forces of the superego and to direct the behavior of the individual. The id, ego, and superego are the three major systems of personality (Hall, 1954). In the healthy person each of the systems performs its task, and the three systems form a unified and harmonious organization. The function of the id is to provide for the discharge of psychic energy that builds up due to stimulation. The superego operates as the moral branch of personality and has the function to strive for perfection rather than pleasure. The ego moderates between the pleasure-seeking of the id and the perfection-seeking of the superego so that the individual can live and operate in reality. It directs behavior so that desires can be fulfilled in the real world in which the individual operates and in a way which will not produce maladjustments. In Freud's sense the ego is similar to the self with an emphasis on the dynamic, directing qualities of the self. While many of Freud's ideas seem to elude empirical testing, they have had a lasting effect on clinical psychology, and many of Freud's pupils have given emphasis to the ego or self even when they have broken with other ideas advocated by their mentor. There are good summaries of Freud's work including ones by Hall (1954) and Brown (1961). Also, many of Freud's works have been published in paperback (Freud, 1963).

Ideas and theories concerning the self and self-concept have developed rapidly during this century. Theorists in this area might be classified into three broad groups. Some have ideas which are variations of the Freudian approach. Members of this group have all placed heavy emphasis on the psychodynamic role of personality, i.e., that personality systems are dynamic energy systems operating within the individual. In this light the ego is seen as the efficient organizer and maintainer of balance (Lowe, 1961).

A second group of theorists have approached self-concept from a humanistic point of view. They assume that man naturally strives for those things that are most conducive to personal growth and self-fulfillment. Two theorists who exemplify this approach to self-concept are Carl Rogers and A. H. Maslow.

According to Rogers (Rogers, 1951) each individual has a basic tendency to strive, to actualize, maintain, and enhance himself. The individual who develops a self which is uniquely his own is a "fully functioning person." In the process of becoming a fully functioning person the individual moves from facades and external evaluations and motivations to a greater awareness of and dependence upon the internal self as an evaluator and motivator. Helping persons to attain this type of functioning has been one of the major goals of therapy patterned after Roger's ideas. Rogers himself sees this type of functioning as a goal for all human interactions. He says:

> On the basis of my experience I have found that if I can help bring about a climate marked by genuineness, prizing, and understanding, then exciting things happen. Persons and groups in such a climate move away from rigidity and toward flexibility, away from static living toward process living, away from dependence toward autonomy, away from being predictable toward an unpredictable creativity, away from defensiveness toward self-acceptance. They exhibit living proof of an actualizing tendency.
>
> Because of this evidence I have developed a deep *trust* in myself, in individuals, and in groups, when we are exposed to such a growth-promoting climate (Rogers, 1973).

A. H. Maslow was primarily concerned with the process of "self-actualization" in psychologically healthy individuals (Maslow, 1954). Many of his ideas about self-actualization, that is, the process of becoming what one has the potential to become, have dealt with a theory of human motivation. Maslow's theory of motivation postulates that individual needs are arranged in a hierarchy. When the need which is lowest in the hierarchy is satisfied, then the next highest need emerges and presses for satisfaction. The assumption is that each person has five basic needs which are arranged as follows:

The thrust of Maslow's work has been to look at healthy, developing individuals to see how they become self-actualizing and to see what characteristics distinguish them.

A third group of psychologists have approached self or self-concept by concentrating primarily on the cognitive dimensions of self. Two theorists who exemplify this approach are G. A. Kelly and J. C. Diggory.

Kelly's (1955) theory, which he calls a psychology of personal constructs, places heavy emphasis on the unique way in which each individual views his world. It is his conviction that man creates his own ways of seeing the world in which he lives. The patterns which man creates and then fits over the realities of which the world is composed are called "personal constructs." Individuals then operate in ways which will seek validation of the constructs which they have built to interpret the world. The psychology of personal constructs has a wide application and has been explicated in a rigorous theory building form by Kelly. While Kelly does not postulate a self-concept, his ideas have had an influence in showing that the self-concept can be viewed as a personal cognitive construction of the individual (Epstein, 1973).

J. C. Diggory (1966) has placed primary emphasis on the way in which individuals evaluate themselves and, in pursuing this line of research, has attempted to apply experimental techniques to the study of self. Diggory regards self as a type of reflexive relation; that is, self is characterized by relationships in which the individual or some part of the individual is both the subject and the object. Diggory's research has concentrated on situations in which individuals evaluate themselves. Diggory has attempted to specify the formal logical operations which are a part of such relationships and has placed heavy emphasis on competence as an aspect of self-esteem. Perhaps the main contribution which Diggory has made is to show that areas of self-concept can be investigated in controlled scientific settings.

Each of the approaches to self-concept and self has added to the understanding of human behavior and the role which self-concept plays in that behavior. The emphasis of the Freudian approach on the dynamic qualities of self has pointed out the necessity for looking at self-concept, not only as a product of what others do to an individual, but also as a determiner of what the individual does. The assumption of the humanistic theorists of the possibilities for human growth and attainment has emphasized the need for schools and other organizations in which children operate to develop growth facilitating environments. The rigor and experimental methods of those in the cognitive group of theorists hold promise for developing more detailed explanations of the mechanisms by which the self-concept is developed and maintained.

Summary

The self-concept is a unique factor in human experience and a powerful influence on human behavior. The self-concept operates to give individuals some internal consistency through a set of expectations and as an interpreter of present and past experiences. The self-concept also is related positively to other desirable characteristics. Of particular interest to the teacher is the positive relationship between self-concept and achievement, reading, and self-responsibility for success and failure and the negative relationship between self-concept and anxiety and prejudice. Of crucial importance to the development and maintenance of self-esteem is the relationship between internal language and self-concept. In addition to the investigation of self-concept by looking at related variables, some psychologists have attempted to explain human behavior using theories involving self-concept. William James and Sigmund Freud stand out as early influences in this area. Carl Rogers and A. H. Maslow are representatives of a humanistic approach to self-concept, and George Kelly and James Diggory have influenced self-concept research by emphasizing the cognitive dimensions of self. In the next chapters, the development and maintenance of positive self-concept will be explored.

Chapter 2

The Development of Self-Esteem

Villiam James said, "Whenever two people meet there are really six people present—there is each man as he sees himself, each man as the other sees him, and each man as he really is." Although these different people are usually somewhat similar, there are differences in the views that individuals have of themselves, in the way others see them, and in the way each really is. The development of self-esteem centers primarily on the way individuals see themselves and on whether the view each has of himself is positive or negative. The basic questions are: Does he think well or badly of himself? Does he like or dislike himself?

One of the underlying assumptions in this book is that it is better to like and to think well of oneself than it is to dislike or think badly of oneself. Although there are occasions when individuals should dislike some of their specific behaviors and reactions, the general evaluation an individual makes of himself should be positive. In a sense, an individual's general evaluation is like an umbrella over all of his everyday behaviors.

A friend who had worked with a child-study program in twenty different states said, "One thing is certain. If a child hates himself, nothing else he does is going to be successful." The inability of children who have negative self-concepts to be successful and to operate well in life is one of the pressing problems which confront teachers. In self-concept training workshops, teachers frequently say things such as, "I don't know what to do with Joe. He is smart but somehow he doesn't think he can do the work. No matter what I try, he seems to turn it into a failure." It is this aspect of self-esteem (or the lack of it) upon which this chapter is focused.

Everyday, teachers work with children who come to school with self-concepts that have been formed during infancy. The teacher cannot control the learning that has gone on before the child comes to school, but the teacher is faced with the task of working with the product of this early learning. If the child has a positive self-concept, the teacher has a firm foundation upon which to build. If the child has a negative self-concept, the teacher needs methods for helping the child to develop feelings about himself which will free him to be successful and happy in the school situation. It is assumed that the teacher wants children to be successful and to be happy in the things they are doing. If the teacher did not have this aim, he likely would be in some other profession. Self-concept becomes a central concern because it influences the behavior of the child in so many ways.

This chapter provides the groundwork for what the teacher can do to encourage the development of self-esteem and for what the teacher can do for children who have developed a negative view of themselves.

To Develop Self-Esteem

Esteem can be either a product or a process. As a product, esteem means high regard or a favorable opinion. As a process, it means to regard with respect or affection, to set a value on, and to rate highly (Allee, 1963). In this discussion, esteem is treated primarily as a process. Preferably, children should emerge from the process of self-esteem with a generally favorable opinion of themselves. But an emphasis on the end-product can distract from the process itself. Self-attitudes and self-conceptions are never static but are constantly changing. Therefore, the emphasis must be on how self-attitudes develop and change in the process of building self-esteem.

How do individuals develop the skills necessary to regard themselves with respect? To answer this question, one must consider the components of self-esteem and answer another question: "What are the prerequisites for regarding self with value and respect?" In this chapter, an overview of the child's progress from birth to adolescence will reveal who and what the primary influences on the development of self-esteem are. Emphasis will be placed upon what the classroom teacher can do to build the necessary components for self-esteem into on-going classroom activities.

Stop for a moment and think about yourself. What kinds of feelings make you happy? What kinds of feelings about yourself make you sad? When you scold yourself, why do you do it? When you compliment yourself, why do you do it? As you do this thinking about yourself, you probably come up with a number of different ideas and memories. Most of these will deal with three areas. One area would be feelings that you have about yourself that center upon times and experiences during which you have felt a part of groups or during which you have felt left out. A second set of your feelings about yourself will have to do with times when you have felt that you were accomplishing something or when you felt you were failing at something. And a third set of feelings will have to do with times when you have felt that you were of value and times when you have felt worthless.

Various writers who have dealt with self-concept have emphasized one or more of the areas mentioned above. These three areas form the necessary components of the process of self-esteem. If development lags in any of the three areas, an important part of self-esteem will be missing. Self-esteem is the result of the development of a sense or a feeling of belonging (Erikson, 1963), competence (Diggory, 1966), and worth (Jersild, 1963).

Belonging. Human beings want to belong. Every individual is born into a social setting. If he does not have other human beings around him to care for and nurture him, he dies. Although there is discussion in child-development literature about whether the child in early infancy simply needs stimulation of one kind or another or love and affection, there is agreement that children need to be cared for. If they are not around other humans, they do not survive. Being cared for usually leads to attachments, and every human wants to belong to social groups, whether the social group is two persons or a larger group.

Belonging to a group or to another person in this sense does not mean that another person owns an individual as a piece of property is owned. To belong in the context of self-esteem means that an individual is a part of a group and is accepted and valued by the other members of that group. To belong requires a mutual sense of oneness. For self-esteem to be operative, it is not only necessary that the group regard the individual in this way but that the individual regard himself as belonging. He must see himself as an accepted and valued member of the group.

Feeling Competent. Another important ingredient of self-esteem is competence. Diggory (1966) has argued that the basis for self-evaluation or behavior is *purpose*. In other words, behavior is purposeful, and humans want to accomplish something by their actions. They evaluate themselves on the basis of how efficiently they accomplish what they set out to do. If they are in school, they are likely to evaluate themselves on how efficiently they master the subjects to which they have given their efforts. If they are efficient in accomplishing their tasks, they have positive evaluations.

In his inner, private realm, every individual has feelings of competence. Diggory has argued that the inner, private feelings of individuals are not the proper subject of science because science deals only with those aspects of behavior and other phenomena which are publicly verifiable. But the teacher is not a scientist in the strict sense. He or she is concerned with goals such as enjoyment and satisfaction and therefore is interested in the feelings of individuals. The adult may have difficulty understanding a child's feelings and may have to use behavior, such as what a child says, as evidence of how a child feels. The evidence may sometimes lead the teacher to draw false conclusions. For example, the child may say that he is not trying to do the work because he doesn't care about it. This would lead the teacher to assume that the feeling of the child is one of disinterest. Over a period of time, he may realize that the child cares very much. The child may care so much, in fact, that he will not let himself get involved for fear of failing. Consequently, the evidence from which the teacher can draw conclusions about feelings is fragmentary, tentative, and frequently confusing. But behavior is the only evidence that is available and therefore is valuable for the teacher.

The process of going from experience to decisions based on that experience or even to a description of that experience is not a simple one. People do the mental processes so automatically and so quickly that they forget that the process is extremely complex. Diagram 1 pictures the process steps involved in going from experience to decisions based on that experience.[1]

---

[1] I am indebted to Dr. Jacob Goering of the Institute for Child Study, University of Maryland, for the basic ideas which appear in this analysis in a revised form, including the basis for Diagram 1.

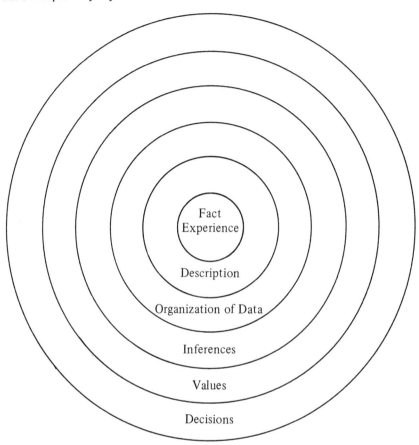

Diagram 1. The Process of Going from Experience to Decisions.

If one were trying to understand another individual and were not limited by space and matter, the best way to understand him would be to live what he is living. It is this idea that is behind statements such as, "Don't criticize a person until you have walked in his shoes for a mile" and "You don't understand because you are not living the life that I am living." When one hears such statements, it is well to admit that they have a measure of truth. People are limited by time, space, and matter and cannot live inside other people. One individual can never see things exactly as another sees them, and two people never have exactly the same experiences and background. Even if one could see the world exactly as another sees it at a particular moment, it would have a different meaning because both had different experiences yesterday and what happened to an individual yesterday changes the meaning he finds today.

When a teacher attempts to understand a student's behavior, he must consider multiple factors, some of which are public and observable and some of which are private and nonobservable. The inner and private factors in a student's behavior, such as feelings and self-perceptions, are not directly accessible to the teacher. Similarly, self-concept is a private dimension. Any information about a student's self-concept the teacher is able to gather is necessarily removed from the actual nature of the self-concept. Teachers are limited to what a student says and does, and, even when a student or any individual makes a sincere effort to be honest and open, there is no way that another individual can observe the internal workings and emotions that make up another's self-concept and lie behind his overt behavior.

The circles in Diagram 1 represent the levels in the process of making decisions based on factual experience. Like the waves made by a rock dropped into a placid pond, the levels of the process started by a specific experience are successively more indefinite as the process progresses outward from the original experience. Eventually, the "waves" of an experience dissipate. The raw experience can be shared with other individuals, but, at each broadening level, the experience becomes more diffused and personal. Sensitive writers are distinguished by their ability to put into words experiences which they have had or have made their characters have, but even the most skillful writers lose something of the experience. C. S. Lewis (1955) argues that, when an individual thinks about an experience, he changes it from raw experience because it is necessary that he attach some meanings to it that are the products of other experiences.

It is not surprising then that an individual cannot express completely his self-concept and inner thoughts about himself. Even his attempts to share it and think about it are changed in the process. The change is not necessarily a negative loss. Hindrances and various negative conceptions can also be changed. It is often said that the past cannot be changed. This is true, but the inference that there is nothing one can do about the past is incorrect. One cannot change the past, but one can change the meaning attached to past experiences. It is not necessary to continue looking at things as one did as a child. Viewpoints can change, and, when they do, it changes the way an individual looks at the past, as well as at the present and the future. This potential for change is important for self-concept development. One of the steps individuals need to take in the process of improving the self-concept is to reinterpret the past so that the meaning of past experiences is changed, especially if the experiences were negative.

Although competence is observable, it should be kept in mind that it is the individual's perceptions of his competence that influence self-esteem. Consequently, the child who has some ability in an objective sense but does not think he has ability is plagued by low self-concept. Since so much classroom behavior deals with competences, the feelings and self-perceptions of competence are important ingredients of self-esteem.

Feeling Worthwhile. The third component of self-esteem is a sense of worth. Statements such as, "I'm no good," "I'm not worth anything to anybody," and "I'm a bad boy" are vocal indications of feelings of worthlessness. Jersild (1952) found that adolescents mention most frequently character and personality characteristics when they describe themselves. This is not unique to adolescents. Adults also tend to think of themselves in terms of "goodness" and "badness," "worth" and "worthlessness." These dimensions have two frames of reference. Individuals see themselves as being worthwhile because of the kind of persons they are and because they see themselves as being worthwhile in the estimation of others. An individual's worth to others is often expressed in what others do for, and to that individual. Feelings of worth in relation to what people do to and for others is one way of looking at love. Fromm (1956) says, "Love is the active concern for the life and growth of that which we love." Individuals perceive that others love them when they perceive that others are doing things to and for them because of active concern for them.

An action which is meant to express love and concern is not always pleasant. A child can distinguish between being bullied by another child and being spanked by an adult who has shown love for him in the past. A child can accept physical punishment from someone who loves him and, at the same time, remember and anticipate more pleasant actions from that person. Unknowingly, the child accepts the punishment as an expression of love—an active concern for his life and growth.

This way of looking at love involves both behavior and feelings. If either feelings or behavior are lacking, the effects or reactions that are expected in situations involving love will be diminished or absent. The parent or the teacher may take action meaning only good for the child, but if the child does not perceive the actions as being out of concern for him, he is not likely to perceive them as evidence of his worth. And if there are expressions of love without appropriate behaviors, the child may also respond negatively. Remember the old joke about the young man who tells his girlfriend that he would climb the highest mountain if she were there, that he would swim a river filled with crocodiles if she were on the other side, that he would brave the stormiest ocean for her presence, and that he would be over to see her on Saturday night if it were not raining. Unless there are behaviors which do in fact express love and worth, the child has nothing to which he can respond. Behaviors which express concern are particularly important for those working directly with children. But in all situations, there is a need for overt actions, both behaviors and words, which show the child the purposes behind what is being done for him and to him. It is crucial for his sense of worth that he perceive actions which express the concern of persons important to him.

It has been assumed in this section that people want to belong, that they want to be competent, and that they want to feel worthy. If this is the case, why do so many children and adults have little or no sense of belonging, competence, and worth? Why are there people, even at a fairly early age, who feel that they are left out, that they are failures, and that they are worthless? These questions center on a basic question: How is self-esteem developed?

Self-Esteem Is Learned

One aspect of self-concept that is agreed upon almost universally is that the self-concept is learned. Individuals are not born with a ready-made self-concept. One may be born with characteristics which will influence the type of self-concept he develops, but the actual development of self-concept is a learned process. Understanding how self-concept is developed through learning is a vital step in investigating why individuals have different learning outcomes in the form of self-esteem or the lack of it.

Although it has been agreed that self-concept is learned, there has been comparatively little research into the learning of self-concept in terms of learning theory. In her exhaustive review of the literature on self-concept, Wylie (1961) found only one study which approached self-concept as a learning theory and then applied the learning theory to self-concept. Although more has been done since 1961 (for example, Gergen, 1971, made an interesting attempt to review the development of self-conceptions in the light of what is known about the learning of attitudes in general), this field is still relatively uninvestigated.

Researchers who have attempted to approach learning from systematic scientific manipulations in a laboratory have often found self-concept too fuzzy. There seem to be too many variables involved, such as feelings, attitudes, desires, etc., which are internal and cannot be controlled in a manner acceptable to an experimental psychologist. The result often has been the elimination of such studies, and there has been a refusal or an inability to look at such areas as self-concept by experimental learning theorists.

On the other hand, psychologists and educators who are interested in the investigation of the growth of wholesome self-concepts have frequently ignored learning theories. They have tended to see learning theories as too restrictive and therefore have either ignored learning theories or looked at them and found them unacceptable. One researcher who is vitally interested in self-concept said, "The trouble with learning theorists is that they don't see that men and rats are very different. In fact, the way most learning psychologists approach people by studying rats, you almost begin to think that men might start growing tails any day."

It would appear that both of these approaches are throwing the baby out with the bath water. If self-concept is important, it needs systematic investigation. And if it is agreed that self-concept is worth investigation and that it is a learned phenomena, it is important to look at ideas about how humans learn. Two generalized conclusions from other learning investigations are helpful in approaching self-concept development. The first is very simple but very basic; it is: People tend to do those things which get them what they want. The second is: People often learn by observation and imitation.

Reinforcement and Self-Concept

People tend to do those things which get them what they want. In other words, when an individual gets something he wants as a result of a particular action, the result of his action reinforces the action. A reinforcer is technically defined as anything which follows a response and increases the probability of that response occurring again. To understand this definition, it may be helpful to look at what occurs in human behavior. Much of human behavior entails responses to elements of the environment. A mother says, "Come here." A child responds by coming to his mother. This type of response is an observable behavior. An individual talks, moves, does something. However, a single behavior usually does not end the sequence of events. Human behavior is usually a series of events. An individual responds with behavior—something happens—he responds in another way—something else happens—and so forth. From the standpoint of reinforcement, it is the "something happens" which is important. Those who have investigated human learning from this point of view have found that the learning acquired is greatly influenced by the consequences of a behavior. Not only is it important to look at what stimulates a behavior, it is important to look at what happens after the behavior. In the example of the child coming to his mother, the consequences of coming to the mother will largely determine how frequently and efficiently the child learns to come to the mother.

There are many possible consequences of a behavior, but these possibilities can be grouped loosely into four categories. The categories of consequences can be: (1) the individual receives something pleasant; (2) something unpleasant is taken away; (3) the individual receives something unpleasant; or (4) something pleasant is taken away. For the earlier example, the child comes to his mother and (1) the mother gives him a hug and kiss; or (2) she removes a sticker that was hurting the child; or (3) she gives him a spanking; or (4) she takes away a toy with which he was playing. Each of these is likely to bring about different "learning." The first two consequences are likely to be reinforcing; that is, they are likely to increase the probability of the child learning to come to his mother. He will tend to come to his mother simply because he enjoys getting hugged, and in fact, he will come at times other than when she says, "Come here."

Remember that for something to be reinforcing it must increase the probability that the behavior will happen again. In this sense, reinforcing a behavior is building it up or making it stronger. It is like reinforcing a wall or a fence. The last two consequences of the behavior, i.e., the mother either spanking or taking something away, are properly called punishment. They are not designed to strengthen a behavior but to eliminate it. The mother is probably looking at what the child has done and is trying to eliminate that behavior to insure that it does not occur again. In this sense, punishment has opposite aims and usually has opposite outcomes than reinforcement.

Two things that build up a behavior have been mentioned. The first is to give something pleasant and is referred to as positive reinforcement. The behavior is reinforced by means of something positive. The second is to take away something unpleasant and is referred to as negative reinforcement. The behavior is reinforced by taking away something negative in character. The distinction between negative reinforcement and punishment is important partly because they are so frequently confused. Some people refer to spankings as negative reinforcement or they say "If he misbehaves, give him a little negative reinforcement." This is an incorrect use of the term. Negative reinforcement is building up a behavior and is done by removing something unpleasant, while punishment is attempting to eliminate a behavior by giving something negative or unpleasant.

Thus far, reinforcement has been approached from a standpoint outside the individual who is actually receiving the reinforcement. In the example of the child-mother interaction, the standpoint was the mother's. Frequently, this is the perspective from which teachers view learning situations. They often ask the question, "If Johnny is doing this, *what can I do?*" For example, "Johnny always jumps up and down during a reading lesson. What can I do to make Johnny sit in his chair and pay attention?" It is useful to try to look at the situation from the standpoint of the individual who is behaving (Stanwyck, Felker, & Van Mondfrans, 1971). It may be well for the teacher to ask, "Why does Johnny do what he does?" From Johnny's point of view the answer would usually be, "Because it gets me what I want."

Skinner, who has done extensive research of reinforcement, refers to most behavior as *operant* behavior. It is behavior that is meant to operate on the environment. Individuals act in purposeful ways and choose actions which will get them to their goals.

When my wife and I were quite a bit younger, we decided that people who smile are more pleasant to be around and have a generally happier life. This was probably because I asked my wife for a first date on the basis that she frequently smiled at me when we met. I did not know at that time that she frequently smiled at everyone. When our first daughter was quite young, we systematically lifted her out of her crib *only* after she had smiled. If she were crying, we attempted to get a smile and then lifted her out of the crib. The results were swift and efficient. She would call or cry. We would come to the crib. She would immediately smile, and frequently interrupting a cry to do so, and then we would immediately lift her out of the crib. From our standpoint, we were teaching her to smile by rewarding her when she smiled. This is the typical parent/teacher viewpoint. But how would my daughter have seen it? From her viewpoint, she was getting us to act in a certain way by using a smile. She had learned that smiling resulted in being picked up, and she quickly learned that a smile is a good instrument. From her viewpoint, the learning was instrumental. She had learned to do something (smile) because it was an effective instrument for getting what she wanted in the environment.

This idea is based on the concept that human beings engage primarily in purposeful behavior, and, if a behavior does not help in reaching the purposes, it is not continued. When looking at behavior, one of the relevant questions becomes, "What is the individual accomplishing by that activity?" One of the particularly powerful accomplishments is positive social response from an important person in the environment.

Most individuals like to have people smile at them and do and say nice things to them. Children like to have a friendly individual show them attention. They will go to great lengths to get attention and will usually respond to smiles, words, and gestures. In fact, the smile is considered by some to be the most pleasureful event that an individual can experience. Schlick, a philosopher, has based his whole system of ethics on the proposition that all humans are motivated to do pleasureful things and that nothing is more pleasureful than another human being's smile. He states, "The happiness of love and the phenomenon of the smile seem to me to be the two most important facts upon which ethics can base itself as upon the firmest data of experience" (Schlick, 1939).

The power of a smile is known to most teachers. According to Horowitz (1967):

> Almost everyone who has interacted with a young child knows that if you laugh at something he does, there is a good chance he will do it again. The adult's laugh serves as a response which has the effect of encouraging the child to repeat his behavior. In this obvious way and in many more subtle ways, adult responses may encourage children to repeat, change, or stop what they are doing.

In addition to this common sense knowledge, there is scientific evidence that social responsiveness can be powerful in learning (see Horowitz, 1967).

When a child acts, the response that he gets can be positive, punishing, or neutral. It would be expected that the child will repeat those behaviors that get positive responses. He would not repeat those that get punishing responses, at least not in the situation where the punishing responses are likely to occur again. In the case of the neutral responses, other activities in the environment will probably determine the probability of repetition. But what about the situation where there is no other person in the immediate environment? What leads a child to repeat many behaviors when there is no adult around? One explanation may be that there is something inherently pleasureful in learning. Simply being able to do something new can serve as reinforcement (White, 1959). It is amazing to watch young children learn a new skill. Recently, I was watching a young foster child in my home learn to walk around a room by holding onto furniture. He tried to take hold of objects over and over and over. And then when he could reach them, he just kept repeating the action until some new task took his attention. He got obvious pleasure from just doing a newly-learned behavior.

Self-Reinforcement

But what role does social reinforcement play in individual activity? Is there something that the individual himself does which could be seen as the counterpart of an adult who gives a child vocal encouragement? In totally individual behavior, the counterpart to what goes on in social interaction may be self-directed speech.

It has been well established that much conversation is private or inner speech in which the individual either vocally or subvocally talks to himself. Inner speech can be used by the individual to direct his behavior in the sense of telling himself what to do. Inner speech can also be criticism and praise of self (see Piaget, 1926, and Kohlberg, Yeager, & Hjertholm, 1968, for a discussion of the power and operations of inner speech).

Children are often observed talking to themselves. A great deal of self-directed speech is done out loud, but as children grow older, it is internalized.

You may be able to recognize your own inner speech as you read. You may find yourself saying things like, "Hm, that is an interesting point" or "This guy is all wet." But your observations are not made out loud. In an uncontrolled observational study with my own children, I attempted to get them to say everything they said to themselves as they worked on a jigsaw puzzle. What they gave was a constant stream of positive, encouraging, direction-giving, and rein- forcing statements. "Oh good, that goes there. Good, I have another one. Schucks, it's getting hard! I can do it. Now I need one with a little hook on one side and a big hook on the other. There it is. Good!" If a teacher had made the same reinforcing statements, he would have been very reinforcing and rewarding, giving a pupil a wealth of positive feedback. But many pupils do not need the teacher's encouragement because they have built positive verbal reinforcement into their own behavior. They maintain their own learning by constantly reinforcing themselves when they accomplish what they set out to accomplish.

The role of inner speech and self-referent language also provides a crucial insight into self-concept. If one looks at self-concept tests, he will find that many of them involve a series of statements to which the child must respond yes or no on the basis of whether he thinks the statement is like him or not like him. As a source for self-concept test items, many of the measures have used Jersild's (1952) collection of statements that people gave to describe what they liked or disliked about themselves. The statements included ones such as:

It is hard for me to make friends.
I am smart.
I am often sad.
It is usually my fault when something goes wrong.
I have good ideas.
I am good in my school work.
I do many bad things.[2]

These statements can be used as an indication of a child's self-concept. Extend this and assume that the child has a similar set of statements which he holds and says to himself. Not only does he think these things about himself, he says them to himself. If this is the situation, there is a built-in reinforcer of the child's view of himself.

Much of what is known about self-concept can be explained by the proposition that the child who has a positive self-concept has learned to give himself positive self-referent verbal feedback and that the child who has a negative self-concept has not learned to do this. The child with a negative self-concept has likely learned to give himself negative verbal feedback or he has not learned to talk to himself and therefore does not give himself much feedback at all.

Self-Reinforcement and Other Characteristics

In Chapter 1, some of the variables to which self-concept is related were discussed. Many relationships have been found and some

---

[2]These are items from the Piers-Harris Self-Concept Scale (Piers and Harris, 1964).

relationships have been found in many different studies, but surprisingly little has been done to try to explain the process or mechanisms which are operating to produce the relationships. Marston has argued that self-reinforcement or positive words and phrases which people say to themselves can provide a bridge between self-concept and learning (1965). This bridge also can be used to show the connection between related variables in self-concept and learning. The proposition that self-concept is developed and maintained by a system of self-referent language has been used to explain many of the previously known relationships between self-concept and other variables (Felker, 1970). For example, the relationship between positive self-concept and low anxiety has been widely verified. If negative self-concept is due partly to a lack of learned ability to give positive verbal reinforcement, an individual with such a deficit is in an ambiguous situation in which he is dependent upon outside forces for reinforcement. The situation is ambiguous because no individual has as much control over how other persons are going to act as he has over how he is going to act. An individual can never be certain whether another person or persons in the environment is going to give him reinforcement in any particular situation. Being placed at the mercy of such an unstable source of reinforcement is an anxiety-producing situation. If the individual has developed an internal system of reinforcement, he can substitute internal reinforcement for external reinforcement, and much of the ambiguity is removed from the situation. He knows that he can be reinforced because he controls the reinforcements. The finding by Felker (1969) that low self-ratings and low peer ratings interact in a relationship with high anxiety is consistent with the idea that an ambiguous source of reinforcements can be a cause of anxiety.

The relationship between self-concept and academic variables also can be explained by the rationale that low self-concept is due partly to an inability to self-administer verbal reinforcements. It has been found that low academic achievement and underachievement are related to low self-concept (Brookover, Thomas, & Paterson, 1964; Coopersmith, 1959; Fink, 1962; Wattenburg & Clifford, 1964). It has been shown also that reinforcement and self-reinforcement are positively related to performance on academic tasks. It would be expected that the pupil who lacks the ability to self-reinforce would have lower performance, and, if such a deficit is also characteristic of low self-concept, the lack of self-reinforcement could explain both the low achievement and the low self-concept.

There is other evidence that the self-referent language approach to self-concept has empirical validity. The rationale has been used to explain known relationships; it has been used to make accurate predictions of relationships between self-concept and other variables (Felker & Thomas, 1971); and it has been used in experimental situations and in a teacher-training setting with confirming results (Felker, 1972; Felker, Stanwyck, & Kay, 1973).

An important advantage of approaching self-concept from the standpoint of language is that it provides the teacher a way of dealing with self-concept development. The problem of how to help children with negative self-concepts is twofold. One aspect of the problem is finding a behavior to begin with. Self-concept involves feelings and perceptions and these are extremely difficult to deal with. How does one change a feeling or a perception? A second aspect of the problem is the fact that teachers are not interested in changing a behavior only. They can easily manipulate a pupil so that he says and does certain things, but in the end, it has been manipulation, and the pupil is still dependent upon the manipulator (Felker, 1972). What is needed is a behavior with which to begin, so that the teacher can deal with it in such a way that it is the individual pupil who is making changes and developing those characteristics and skills which will prepare him to have a happy and fruitful life. Teachers should want to *teach* him, not to manipulate him. Self-referent praise and self-reinforcement open the door for dealing with self-concept in an acceptable and effective way.

Self-Concept and Imitation

The second important learning concept which helps in understanding self-concept development is that individuals often learn by simply watching someone else. People who work with children know from experience that children are copy cats and that children sometimes seem more likely to copy something undesirable by adult standards. It has been found that imitation is an extremely powerful force in learning everything from simple motor tasks to values and cognitive skills (Felker & Milhollan, 1970).

The power of imitation has important implications for self-concept development. Much of the research and writing on self-concept development has used exclusively an approach from the standpoint of what adults actually do to a child. Although the treatment of a child is important, an approach restricted to it overlooks the important influence of how individuals treat themselves. The parent not only does things to the child, the parent does and says things to and about himself in the presence of the child. Similarly, the teacher not only does things to the pupils, he does and says things about himself in the presence of the pupils.

It is important to remember that an individual learns a specific behavior through imitation by seeing someone else do it. If the behavior to be learned is something that is not visible, such as thinking or feeling, with no outward expression, it becomes impossible for the child to imitate. He cannot see what is going on inside the parent or teacher, and, if he cannot see or hear what is going on, he cannot imitate it.

The child is often left to imagine what the important adults around him are thinking or saying to themselves. It is amazing how many things adults assume children have somehow learned which, in fact, adults have given them no opportunity to learn. If you have brothers and sisters who are less than twelve, ask them how much they think your father makes a year. The distortion will amaze you. If you have the stamina, ask a child what he or she thinks you say to yourself when you can't work a problem or when you work a problem and it is wrong.

What you find out by asking children these questions is indicative of the many distortions children pick up when statements and actions are not externalized. Most adults have learned to do many things internally. They have learned not to talk out loud to themselves and not to go around advertising what their salary is. But they have learned this because they live in an adult society where other adults have also learned to internalize many behaviors. When dealing with children, adults must remember that children have not learned to internalize all such behaviors. If children are to learn how they are to treat themselves, they need models who can help them learn by imitation.

The aspects of learning by imitation suggest that the important persons who are around a child have an important influence on self-concept development. Sullivan (1947) initiated the phrase *significant others* to refer to people who play an important part in a child's development. These significant others are influential in learning a self-concept and in learning to self-evaluate. Reinforcement by significant others and modeling after significant others are important factors in learning self-esteem as opposed to self-derogation.

The role of particular significant others changes as the child develops, and various people become significant others at different times in the development of the child and adult. For example, the parents are usually significant others for most of the life of an individual. But in infancy, the parents, particularly the mother, are frequently the total range of significant others. As the infant develops into a child (two years old and older), other individuals enter his life as significant others. He often has brothers and sisters, as well as other relatives, who influence him. Even if he has no siblings, he may eventually have a younger sibling who is significant in his life. As he grows, he has friends. A child at three and a half years may insist on including a list of friends in his prayers in addition to Mommy, Daddy, Grandma, etc.

This steady progression to a larger number of persons who are significant in the life of the child is important for self-concept and self-evaluation. If the child develops an internal system of self-esteem and the mechanisms for maintaining this system, he can meet new people and influences with confidence. If he does not develop a positive system of self-evaluation and self-esteem, the greater number of people who are significant in his life increases the number of people upon whom he is dependent. This dependence increases the ambiguity in his life. Although he may come to depend upon mother as a stable and consistent reinforcer, the child is certain to find that playmates, other adults, etc., are less consistent and reinforcing. Therefore, the importance to the child of developing a strong system of self-reinforcement and self-referent praise as a means of maintaining self-esteem cannot be overemphasized.

When a child goes to school, the range of people and activities open to him is geometrically magnified. He now has at least one teacher with whom he has to relate for a large portion of the day. He also may have a teacher's helper who is another adult. He comes into contact with lunchroom personnel and often has one or more special teachers for art or music. In addition, there are the bus driver, the janitor, the principal, the playground supervisor, the crossing guard, and many other adults. All of these adults are in the position of helping and bossing, of evaluating and instructing. But they are not all. The range of peer contacts is magnified also. From the typical home situation where the child has one or two friends with whom he plays, he is thrust into a situation where he is supposed to get along with twenty or more other children.

Each of these new people has the potential for becoming a significant other in the life of the child. In many cases if he does not choose to regard the people as significant, it will be taken as a sign that he is not getting along well in school. For example, one of my children did not get along with the teacher in her nursery school. When asked why she did not listen to Mrs. So-And-So, she said, "I don't want to listen to her. She does not act like a teacher is supposed to act." The fact was that the teacher did not act like the child's first nursery school teacher had acted, and therefore my daughter determined that the teacher was not a significant other to whom she wanted to pay attention. However, children rarely have this choice. They are put into a school situation with the expectation that they will give some heed to the teacher and that the teacher by his position will be a significant influence on the child. Consequently, there is a lot of pressure on the child to regard the school-related adults as significant others.

Summary

The development of self-esteem in children should be of prime concern to teachers and parents. Self-esteem is cultivated when the child develops a sense of belonging, competence, and worth. The nature and mechanisms of learning are crucial factors in understanding how individuals learn that they belong, are competent, and of worth. Two ideas from the study of the learning process which can aid in understanding self-concept development and enhancement are reinforcement and imitation. It has been suggested that self-reinforcement can provide a bridge between learning theory and self-concept. The learning of self-esteem can be facilitated by those who are significant others in the life of the child.

The most prominent significant others and how they are likely to interact in the learning which the child has to do in the area of self-concept will be discussed in the next chapter. Significant others interact to influence the senses of belonging, competence, and worth which together make up self-esteem.

Chapter 3

The Self-Concept
in Infancy and Childhood

O ne of the most frequent laments of teachers is, "What can we do during the short time we have a child when what is going on at home is working in the opposite direction?" This sometimes is an excuse for not doing what can be done and for not taking responsibility for the task of helping the child to learn and change. The lament does emphasize, however, the crucial fact that no child comes to school a blank tablet. Each child comes with a self-concept, just as each child comes with a set of learnings about the world and the tasks which he will be expected to master in school.

The teacher can help the child with self-esteem master the developmental tasks of formal schooling without damaging his self-esteem. For the child who comes to school with basically negative views of himself, the new learning experiences of school provide the opportunity to reteach the child a view of himself that includes a sense of belonging, competence, and worth. Reteaching a self-view is not an easy task. Research indicates that the self-concept is a stable variable (Stanwyck, 1972). Therefore, it is difficult to change. But those times during life when other new learnings are going on would seem to offer the type of fluid situation in which new learning about self could take place.

In this chapter, we will concentrate on the development of self-concept during infancy and early childhood. These early years are preschool and you might wonder why a chapter on preschool children is included in a book primarily intended for teachers. If teachers are going to help children develop positive views of themselves and help some children change the views which they have of themselves, teachers will find it helpful to look at some of the important phases of development which have come before school. The discussion of the preschool years will not be exhaustive, but there will be an attempt to point up the type of significant interactions which influence self-concept development in the early years so that you can be better able to see the results of such development in the children who come into your class each day.

Parents and Self-Concept

In the first two years of a child's life, the parents of a child are a significant influence on the development of self-concept in at least three basic ways: The parents serve as the primary models for the developing behavior of the child; the parents serve as the primary feedback agents so that the child can know how his behavior is influencing others; and the parents serve as the primary evaluator of the behavior of the child. Most people who work with children agree that the mother is more influential than the father during infancy. The mother usually spends more time with the infant and usually has the major responsibility of caring for the physical needs of the infant. Parents who operate on widely different assumptions and whose behaviors are significantly different from each other present the child with a set of problems. Assume for this discussion that the mother and father agree on the general way in which children should be treated and that their behavior toward the child, although not identical, is at least not widely divergent.

The parents, or the parent figures in situations where there is no natural parent, influence the sense of belonging, the sense of competence, and the sense of worth through his or her behavior and role as model, feedback agent, and evaluator. The early learning of the child is strongly influenced by the primary model figure who is available to him. Some psychologists have attempted to explain the whole process of identification (the emotional attachment of a child to his parents and the adoption of the parents' behaviors and values as his own) by attributing this process to imitation (Bandura & Huston, 1961; Kagan, 1958). The model that the parents present in their treatment of the child and in their treatment of themselves and each other teaches the child how he should treat himself.

For example, children frequently come to parents and make statements using the same words and inflections that the parents have used when talking to the child. "I'm a good boy. I went to the potty all by myself" is likely to sound very much like the parent who has previously said to the child, "You are a good boy. You went to the potty all by yourself."

Each individual receives multiple feedback cues from the environment, and some of these cues are provided in the interactions of the individual with his environment. Individuals do things, and the consequences or outcomes of the actions provide their own feedback. The child attempts to ride a bicycle and falls. The facts that the bicycle ends up on the ground and that his knee hurts provide him with natural feedback on his activities.

A second type of feedback requires that another human agent operate in the situation. The parent operates as a feedback agent. Much of the feedback from parents and other humans to infants gives "moral" or "worth" meaning to the results of the activities. The boy who knocks over a lamp receives immediate feedback on his competence in the sense that the lamp falls and breaks. It takes another human in the situation to add the dimension of *morality* or *worthiness*. This dimension is added in such statements as, "you are a good boy!" or "you are a bad boy!" Notice that both of these statements do not deal directly with the boy's behavior. Even though the statements may have been brought about by a lamp-knocking-over incident, they have gone beyond the behavior and have attached meanings of worth to the individual.

A few years ago my family had a four-year-old foster child in our home for a few months. He would react to situations in which he felt that he had done something which he should not have done by sitting and slapping his hand and saying out loud to himself, "You are a bad boy! You are a bad boy!" The feedback agent in his early life had not only given him information which he had accepted as being accurate and correct, i.e., that he was in fact a bad boy, but had also presented him with a powerful model for his actions toward himself in such situations. The response which he imitated was hitting his hand and voicing his displeasure with himself by saying, "You are a bad boy!" One of the things which parents frequently do.

which reinforces the types of self-hate and self-punishment which are seen in children with negative self-concepts is to say something to a frustrated and angry child such as, "Why get angry with me (or the chair, or the lamp, or the teacher)? The person you should be angry with is yourself. You got yourself in this mess." The child needs to learn self-responsibility in an atmosphere which includes help in adequately managing the responsibility. The child who is in a situation which he has not been able to handle receives double blows if he is forced to abuse himself and take his anger out on himself.

The parent figure also acts in the role of an evaluator. Although the child can receive a natural evaluation of his efforts by observing what happens when he attempts something, the adults in the situation many times provide a verbal evaluation. "That is very good!" "You can't do it." "What a big boy!" Adults have many such verbal evaluations that they give to children. One of the difficulties which parents face is that, as a general rule, children of all ages want to do many things which are too advanced for them. But unfortunately, parents frequently do not want their children to do many things which the children are perfectly capable of doing. The child wants to climb to the top of the tree, which is probably a little too high and difficult for coming back down, and the worried mother does not want the child to climb the tree at all for fear that he will fall. The child wants to put his own spinach into his mouth (or at least a portion of it), and the mother continues to feed him because he can only partly handle the spoon. Too frequently, adults give negative evaluation rather than positive teaching. My sister-in-law provided a classic example of the positive way to handle this type of situation. One morning, her young daughter had climbed the steps about five times and then sat at the top of the stairs crying because she did not know how to come down. After going up five times to bring her down, her mother said, "I'm going to put a stop to this! Tomorrow I'm going to teach her how to come down steps."

Belonging, Competence, and Worth

While the parent is learning how to use his or her role as model, feedback agent, and evaluator in a positive sense, the infant is faced with the early learnings of belonging, competence, and worth.

The infant is faced with the conflict between pain and comfort. He wants comfort (which is probably a universal desire only overruled when humans are able to evaluate other desires), and yet he is dependent on those around him for this comfort. He cannot change his own pants; he cannot get his own food; he cannot burp himself. In this sense, he is "executively incompetent" (Ausubel, 1957). He cannot execute his desires or carry a sequence of behavior through until a need is satisfied through that behavior. But this fact does not stop him from desiring things, and, in most situations in Western culture, it does not prevent him from having those desires fulfilled. The desires of the infant seem to be minimal—he wants to be fed, dry, and cuddled. Most families provide these three enjoyments in life and even go out of their way to make sure that they are present before the infant experiences any intense degree of pain or discomfort.

Psychologists have argued about whether the identification of the child with the parents is due to the force which they can exert in the form of punishment or whether it is due to the love which they show by meeting the child's needs. The argument may be academic in the sense that there is evidence that either situation will produce an identification of the child with the parent and that the identification of the child will be strongest where both situations are present (Kagan, 1958).

The identification of the child with the parent so that the child adopts the behaviors and ideas of the parent as his own provides the child with an indication of where he belongs and to whom he belongs in the world. The child is faced with two primary tasks in the early infant years. One is the problem of security. Where can I feel secure in this world? This problem is solved by a strong attachment to the parents who are obviously more powerful than the infant. The parents usually are more powerful in the life of the child than any other humans. The second problem is that of status. How do I gain a position of status and power in this life? The question of power may seem a little premature, but Ausubel (1957) argues that the infant is faced with a struggle for power with the parents. In early infancy, the parents give the child everything he desires, and yet, as his ability to do things for himself increases, the parents increasingly put restrictions on his actions. Most parents have seen this process. They can allow the child to have almost everything he wants as long as he is very young, but, when he learns to walk and climb, of necessity they put some types of restrictions on the activities of the child. There are some "dos" and some "don'ts" which are enforced. When the enforcements begin (usually when the child starts to walk and increasingly as he begins to talk), the child is faced with the question—"How can I continue to see myself as a powerful individual in the light of all the restrictions and greater power of my parents?" The process of identification also answers this question. The child who identifies and attaches himself to the parents is in a sense adopting the old adage—"If you can't beat them, join them."

The process of identification leads to a number of important outcomes for self-concept. One outcome is that it provides a sense of belonging. The child attaches himself to the parent and begins to make himself like the parent. The role of the parent as a model is magnified, and the strength of imitation is increased. The second important outcome is that the sense of belonging provides both a secure place so that the child knows that he is safe and can operate from this safety without fear. This place of security also gives the child a measure of self-perceived power since the wishes of the parents now become the wishes which he adopts.

Achieving a sense of belonging is one of the earliest tasks which the child has to accomplish. The process of identification continues beyond the infant years. The security which the child feels in early infancy from having his needs met and the safety that he feels in experiencing comfort instead of pain provides the basis on which identification builds. The sense of belonging also provides the foundation on which the child can build an early sense of competence.

One of the struggles which humans face throughout life is between competence and incompetence. This struggle is intensified in pre-adulthood by the fact that the child is always incompetent, because he is always faced with learning tasks. Much learning is going on in early childhood. Almost by definition, the child is incompetent in those tasks which have not yet been learned. Actually, the struggle throughout life is not so much between being competent as opposed to being incompetent but in perceiving oneself in a positive way in spite of the incompetencies which may be present. The example referred to in Chapter 1 about John Adams is an illustration of an individual who continued to look only at his incompetencies rather than at his competencies and the possibilities of growth that were present.

The infant must begin the task of looking at incompetencies as learning tasks rather than as personal defects or personal fate. "You can't do it now but you will be able to do it!" should be the almost constant reaction of the parent to the child's incompetencies.

Recently, I was watching my son try to climb up on a chair. If you have ever taken the time to see how adults sit in a chair, you have seen what an interesting process it is. Adults stand with their backs to the chair, sort of back into the chair, and then sit down. But what do you do when your legs are not tall enough for your seat to reach the chair when you go through this process? This incompetency was frustrating my son when he was younger. He would back up to the chair and try to hump his seat up to the chair. He was not successful, and it was making him very angry. I showed him how to get up on the chair by climbing on the rungs, putting his knees on the seat, and then turning around and sitting after he had climbed up. But this still did not satisfy him. He said, "No! Daddy's way." He was not satisfied until I took him to the full-length mirror and showed him how tall my legs were and how tall his were. I explained how his legs were going to grow until they were tall enough to reach the chair and that this would not be too long, but he would have to climb up the other way until then. He was satisfied. Now that my son is older, I am working on breaking his habit of climbing on the rungs by helping him learn to go directly to the seat with his knees.

The fact that infants lack the competence which they will acquire later and which they see in older persons around them is partly offset by the fact that learning occurs in rapid sequence. Just as infants and children receive much feedback of incompetence, they also receive continual feedback of new competencies. As individuals progress from childhood toward adulthood, they go through the process with increasing competencies but decreasing amounts of new learning. They have more evidence of being able to accomplish tasks and less evidence of learning new ones. If the child is going to develop a sense of competence, important people around him should emphasize the new things that he has learned and the possibility of additional learning rather than the amount of incompetence he exhibits.

The young infant also begins to achieve a sense of worth. Early parental care for the infant contributes to this sense of worth by showing the infant that the parents are attuned to his needs. The fact that parents will act to give comfort instead of pain tells the infant that he is of worth. The infant also receives confirmation that he is of value and worth in the sight of his parents by the verbal and physical expressions of love which they show him. These are indirect ways of saying, "You are worthwhile."

Perhaps the most prevalent and long-lasting influence on the development of a sense of worth in the child is the learning of language. Much of the language which the child uses will be self-referent. Children learn the use of pronouns at about two years of age (McCarthy, 1954). They also learn early that their name stands for them. It is rather interesting that the reaction of a child to his name is a valid and reliable indication of his self-concept (Boshier, 1968). If the child likes his name, he tends to like himself, and, if he dislikes his name, he tends to dislike himself. It is impossible at this point to say whether the attitude toward the name comes first or whether the child in fact learns to dislike himself and then attaches these self-attitudes to the verbal symbol which stands for him. Self-referent words such as "me" can have meanings to the individual that are different from the meanings given to such terms by the group in which the individual finds himself. One way to change the behavior of the individual is to change the meanings which he attaches to words describing important persons and behaviors (Clayson, 1969).

In addition to the meanings which the child attaches to names and other self-referent terms, he also learns a body of self-referent language which he uses when he talks to himself. He learns things such as, "I can do it," "I am a good boy," and "I am a bad boy." It is interesting to watch children and to discover that they first learn to use words and later learn to attach meanings to them. The fact that children imitate words, even in situations where the words appear to be used correctly, does not mean that they have attached all of the meanings to these words that the adults in the situation attach.

My youngest son frequently heard my daughters say, "Mom, can I help you make cookies?" One day when none of the girls were home, my wife said that she was going to make cookies. Jeffrey said, "Mom, can I help make cookies?" She replied, "No, I don't think so. I'm in too much of a rush right now." Jeff replied, "Oh goody, I don't want to work right now!" He had learned the words and had used them in a situation where they seemed appropriate. The words, however, did not have connotations that his sisters in the same situation had given to them. The same is true of self-referent words. The early use of self-referent language is an opportunity for adults to notice and correct the use of those self-referent terms and phrases to which the child is likely to attach a weight of negative meanings in the normal course of development.

I mentioned previously the boy who sat in the corner and slapped his hand and said, "I'm a bad boy." This boy also sat with toys and said, "I can't do it!" He would then try to convince an adult in the situation to do it for him. There was an accumulation of evidence that indicated that activities which he had been taught to do he could do with a high degree of coordination and skill. For example, he could dribble a basketball at age four and could make a fair percentage of baskets in the clothes basket. We picked an activity in which he appeared to have no experience—wooden puzzles. My wife or I sat on the floor with him and guided his hands so that the piece fell into place. We then clapped our hands and said, "Joe, did it! Joe can do it!" Then we worked with him on another piece until it fell into place and repeated the whole process. When we began the process, the most common statement that Joe made was "Joe can't do it." After a few weeks, he began to do the puzzle on his own, and, when we did not see him and clap, he came and showed us so that we would clap. A few weeks later, he was sitting and doing his own clapping and saying each time, "Joe can do it!" He even taught his younger brother that this was the way to go about working puzzles. This seems like a simple example, and it probably was not a life-changing incident. But it did generalize to other activities, and it is deceptively simple.

The idea behind such use of self-referent encouragement is complex and has tremendous force in human life. Humans learn the meaning of things and attach these meanings to words. The words then serve to carry the full weight of the meanings of experience and life. Words that children learn are with them long after some of the basic experiences which attached meanings to those words have been forgotten. It is this enduring quality which makes the development of self-referent language so powerful. Teaching children to use positive self-referent language and helping them to attach positive meanings to the verbal symbols is a vital part of self-concept development.

Self-Concept and the Toddler

When the child reaches the period of approximately 18 to 36 months of age, a number of rapid changes take place. Dramatic changes take place in the degree of executive competence he has attained. He can walk; he can usually feed himself; he has mastered a number of words; and he has begun to put these words together into the true language of sentences and phrases. He is about to begin or may have already learned control of toilet behaviors. Once these tasks are completed, the child enters a rather dramatic new phase in his life. He is no longer a baby! Adults who are around him expect him to act like a child, and, at this stage, the child is eager to step into the role of a big boy or a big girl.

Although the family continues to be the primary source of important others, the child also begins to learn that there is more to the world than his family. Rather than spending time playing alone or following mother around the house, he likes the company of other children. He is able to play by contributing to the interaction rather than simply being "played with."

This new realm of activity outside of the family also brings with it continued self-concept development. The sense of belonging, competence, and worth which the child has developed must be adjusted to take into account the child's experiences.

The child's sense of belonging must take into account the fact that he belongs to more than a family. He must learn that he belongs to a group of friends and to a world that is larger than the family. The child must also learn that the world is a good place or, unfortunately for some, that the world is a bad place.

The sense of belonging is enlarged to include the fact that people out there like the child or dislike him. A friend of mine has frequently pointed out that children differ greatly in their sympathy-getting ability. There are some children that you just want to reach out to and help because they are so attractive. But there are other children who, to you at least, are not nearly so attractive. They would be expected to have a more difficult time feeling that the world is friendly and kind to them. Developing these feelings and perceptions is a part of the continuing development of the sense of belonging.

Another primary task which becomes important in this period of the child's development is that of sexual identity. The child learns that he is a boy or a girl and in this process gets another perspective on where he or she belongs in the world. Although the process of sex-typing continues for some years, it seems to be particularly active in the infant and adolescent periods. In the infant period, the child learns a basic set of appropriate behaviors and learns to inhibit a set of behaviors that are inappropriate by his society's standards. In many situations, girls are taught to be ladylike and taught not to play rough games or to fight. Boys are taught that they are to be strong and that they are not to play with dolls. Although these kinds of learnings and teachings are very subtle, there is considerable evidence that they are effective.

The process of sex-typing or of learning the differences between male and female behavior begins early. By age two years, children can identify male activities as being "male" with a high degree of accuracy (Silcock, 1965). At age two and a half years, children can identify items by appearance and task according to sex linkage at 75 percent accuracy for both male and female items (Vener & Snyder,

1966), and, by age three, they can judge a wide range of activities according to sex appropriateness (Schell & Silber, 1968). Sex differences in preferred play activities and in actual play also are noted by age three (Fagot & Patterson, 1969).

When the child attends school, the factor of appropriate masculine or feminine behavior exercises a vital influence. This influence seems to affect boys more than girls, and the influence is in conflicting directions. On the one hand, the early elementary boy needs male behaviors to succeed (Anastasiow, 1965). Boys who are highly masculine in their behavior are rated higher by teachers on a number of dimensions and show higher achievement scores than boys with median or low masculine behaviors. On the other hand, teachers consistently reinforce behaviors which are feminine in the classroom setting (Fagot & Patterson, 1969). This presents the male child with a conflict situation. Girls are not faced with the same conflict because the teacher does not reinforce cross-sex behaviors for girls.

The process of learning appropriate sex behavior is usually facilitated or retarded by the parents who act as models. This factor has been studied primarily with children who have a parent absent from the home. Since there are more families where the father is absent than families where the mother is absent, most of the research has been done on the influence of the father absence from the home, and little is known about the effects of mother absence. In general, it has been found that father absence from the home has a disadvantageous effect on boys (Biller, 1969; Santrock, 1970). The disadvantageous effect of father absence is moderated by the time of absence. If the father is present until the boy is five years old, the effect of later absence appears to be minimal (Hetherington, 1966). Other factors, such as length of absence, relative availability of male surrogate models, and individual differences in the female model, need to be taken into account (Biller, 1970).

Being an only child in the family with an absent father seems to have the most depressing effect on achievement, particularly in the early and middle years (Sutton-Smith, Rosenberg, & Landy, 1968). The fact that father absence influences the development of male children indicates that the effects of modeling are crucial in sex-typing. If the father is not present in the home, both male and female personality development is likely to be characterized by increased femininity (Summers & Felker, 1970). In general, the findings support the role of modeling in the development of sex-appropriate behavior (Heilbrun, 1965).

The child who does not develop the characteristics which society

labels at any particular time as male or female is faced with a wealth
of feedback which indicates to him that he does not belong. The boy
who has long hair or short hair, whichever is in opposition to the
current societal stereotype of maleness, is faced with an image which
is out of harmony with the prevailing stereotypes. A similar process
operates with all physical characteristics which are sex-stereotyped.
The girl who is taller than the majority of boys or the boy who is
shorter than most of the girls must deal with a stereotyped characteristic and develop an adequate sense of belonging. Numerous other
physical characteristics, such as facial hair, secondary sex characteristics, voice range, etc., carry societal stereotypes of maleness or
femaleness and become important at adolescence.

Although these physical characteristics are difficult for the child,
it is perhaps more difficult for the child to deal with emotions and
desires which are judged inappropriate for his sex. Girls who are
angry and aggressive not only must deal with the behavior but must
handle the feedback that labels them "tomboys." The boy who is
fearful is not only dealing with the emotion but with the constant
feedback that he is "like a girl." The sense of identity and belonging
is a part of self-concept and gives the child a sense of belonging to a
group, in this case, the group of males or females. This differentia-
tion of where he fits is a prelude to being an autonomous member of
the group.

The child's sense of competence is likely to be enlarged in the preschool years. He is more frequently with peers, and his competencies
are evaluated not only by the members of his family but by age
mates. During the preschool years, the child is introduced to something which he will face throughout high school; that is, he must face
getting fairly harsh evaluations from age mates because his age mates
have not reached the level of maturity required to temper criticisms
on the basis of the needs of other individuals.

The sense of competence is also confused in the preschool period,
because competence begins to become enmeshed with competition.
There is a strong drive, which usually is magnified later by the school
system, to judge competence on a competitive basis. Judgments and
evaluations in infancy are usually made on the basis of, "How am I
doing in comparison to how I did yesterday." As the child expands
his range of contacts with other children, adults frequently change
the basis of evaluation. The judgments begin to be made on the basis
of how well the child does in comparison to other children, not in
comparison to his past self. Even though adults "know" that children
develop at different rates and that it is not reasonable to expect all

children to perform at the same level or to do things at the same time, there is a strong tendency to compare children with each other. These comparisons change the basis for the sense of competence and make the maintenance of the sense of competence a difficult and unpleasant experience for many preschoolers.

The enlargement of the sense of competence brings problems when the child ventures more into the world. But the enlarged area in which the child operates also allows the possibility of some major encouragement for the sense of competence. The child has a larger set of evaluators and feedback agents. He receives information from other adults and other children. Even though this feedback information may be destructive, the increased feedback means that the number of positive evaluations also can be increased. This is particularly important in situations where the parents have unrealistic expectations for the child and have built these expectations on an inaccurate knowledge of the child's capabilities. When their child begins to operate with other children, the parents may begin to see that their evaluations have been too critical, and they may change their basis for evaluation and feedback to the child.

The enlarged area in which the sense of competence can develop also gives the child more opportunity for natural feedback of competence information. When the child is playing outside the home, he or she is more independent of the direction of the parents and therefore has a much wider range of things to try. With the opportunity to try more things, there is a greater natural feedback of increased competence. Most parents have breathed a sign of relief when the child says, "Guess what we did today?" and then found that it was something that the child did successfully and without harm but that it was probably something they would have told the child not to do if they had known about it ahead of time. But the point is, he did it successfully and he would not have been able to try it if he had not moved out into the larger arena of playing without the direction of an adult.

Having playmates also increases the range of competence. My four-year-old boy was playing with a friend who was allowed in the garage to get toys, but he always had to ask his mother to open the garage door. He and my son Jeff found a bucket. One of them held the other while he balanced on the bucket and turned the garage door handle. Then the two of them pushed the garage door up. I asked him what they did next and he said, "Well, he helped me stay on the bucket and pull the door down so we could try to open it again!" Children learn to do things together which they cannot do individually, and they also learn new behaviors by imitating each other. The child in the infancy period is restricted to imitating the parents or siblings or television, but the child in the preschool period is usually in touch with a wider range of models, including playmates, and has more opportunities for expanding his competencies.

The use of language is another important aspect of increased competence. Although formal language and reading training are delayed for many children until school age, for others learning to read and to enjoy the magic of books is developed in the preschool years. This not only provides the child with increased tools with which to operate on the environment, it provides him with a wider range of models and with greatly increased opportunities for gaining competencies.

Summary

The primary contributors to a sense of worth during the infant period are the parents. The care which the child receives serves as evidence that he is of worth to those who are doing the caring. The security that he receives from a sense of belonging also signifies to him that someone thinks he is special. As the child moves into a wider environment, his sense of worth is vested to a greater degree in the competence he acquires. Diggory (1966) argues that individuals maintain a system of self-evaluation and self-worth that is instrumental. According to Diggory, they view themselves as worthwhile if they are efficient instruments in achieving their goals. This process of basing their worth on their ability to do things is accelerated by moving out of the home situation and operating more frequently in the wider world. During the preschool period, the child begins to judge his self-worth partly on the basis of his competence with objects, his competence with peers, and his competence with adults. The child who has not developed a sense of belonging and the security that accompanies such a sense is likely to be hindered in moving out into the wider world. Security provides the basis for the confidence that the child can meet the world without excessive fear. Once he steps out into the wider world, the competence which he develops will tend to enhance the beginnings of positive self-esteem. The fearfulness and lack of confidence which prevent some children from developing competence will reinforce the beginnings of a negative self-concept.

The infant and preschool period provides the basic self-evaluation and self-concept learnings that the child brings to the school situation. When children come to school, teachers want them to feel secure. This security should lead to a sense of belonging and a feeling that they will be accepted as a part of the social group in which they find themselves. Teachers also want them to develop a sense of competence so that they can approach learning situations with the confidence that they will become competent even though they may be incompetent at the beginning. Teachers want the child to view himself as being worthy not only because he can do things and master tasks but because those around him have taken care of him in a manner which shows that he has worth in their eyes.

Chapter 4

Self-Concept Enhancement in Elementary School Years

Parents set the stage, but the play is acted out with peers, teachers, and bosses.

Boyd R. McCandless

The mother who cries when her "baby" goes to school for the first day is an emotional prophet. She will probably rejoice in the growth and development of the child, but the step out the door on the way to school is one of the major factors in changing from dependence to independence. The dependence relationship between parent and child becomes impossible after the child enters into the new world of school.

The changes brought about by starting school are dramatic both for mother and child, and the changes are of tremendous importance in the development of the child. The changes brought about by school-child interactions produce new and exciting consequences in the development and enhancement of the child's self-concept.

Once the child goes to school he gains increased independence. Although the child has moved in the preschool years to a wider world than he found in infancy, he or she remained largely under the supervision of the parents. In fact, many children during the preschool years begin to think that the mother and father are omnipotent (all-powerful) and omniscient (all-knowing). Parents, in many cases, foster the child's thinking that the parent knows everything by not revealing to their children how the parents get their knowledge. For example, a mother may ask, "Johnny, why were you in the cookie jar?" without telling Johnny that the crumbs on his lips and the tilted cookie jar lid gave him away; or, "Johnny, why were you in the garage?" without telling him that Mrs. Jones had mentioned that she saw the children playing in the garage. The parent picks up enough clues from the preschooler to keep close track of what he is doing. Such surveillance is impossible once the child has entered school. The child does many things which his parent does not know about and begins to recognize that every move is not seen by his parent. This independence allows more exploration and also places a greater emphasis on the self. The child is increasingly in charge of himself, and consequently, more and more evaluations of behavior are going to be self-evaluations, and a greater percentage of his rewards are going to be self-rewards.

The child also meets a new primary model, feedback agent, and evaluator—the teacher. The change in persons who occupy the role of model and evaluator from the parents to the teacher is an important factor in the child's independence. Parents face the futile task of trying to convince a young child that something which he knows the teacher said is incorrect. In many of these situations, the teacher's word becomes law, and the simple, "But Dad, Miss Jones said that this is so!" becomes the last meaningful sentence in an argument.

The fact that the child has an alternate source of rewards and an alternate model also frees the child to test the omnipotence and omniscience of the parent. One of the more frequent tests is a simple question such as "Dad, is the moon 250,000 miles away from the earth?" The unsuspecting father answers, "That sounds reasonable, why?" An answer which brings the scornful response, "No, it's not. It is 238,857 miles away." The wary father soon learns to admit ignorance from the beginning rather than having it proved to him. The new independence may be seen in the statement like "But Mom, Miss Jones said that we were not to ask our parents to help us with math since they probably would only confuse us. Things have changed so much since you were in school!"

School life adds pressures in addition to providing alternate sources of rewards and evaluations. Anxiety is likely to be associated with those areas to which much social value is attached, and, consequently, anxiety is likely to be attached to the school situation.

It has been found that there is a general increase on the part of a significant number of students in negative attitudes toward school. The increase in negative attitude is seen not only in increasing negativism as the children progress through school grades (Dunn, 1968) but as they go from the beginning to the end of the school year (Flanders, Morrison, & Brode, 1968).

The pressure of school and the resulting anxiety are partly due to the fact that the child is thrust into a situation which is highly evaluative and over which he exercises very little control. There is evaluation by parents, peers, and the general environment outside of school, but these evaluations are not as systematic or pervasive as the evaluations which are a continual part of the school environment. It would be interesting to tabulate how many times the child, in the normal school day, does something which is evaluated either directly by a verbal statement or indirectly by everyone in the group doing the same thing. Even if the typical school system had no grades, there would still be the evaluation that is a consequence of external goals being set up and a product being produced which either meets or does not meet the external goals.

The fact that the goals of school are external is an important aspect of pressure and anxiety for the child. In most situations, the child has little to say about suggestions, requirements, and emphases during the school day. Society and the teacher, as the representative of society, have a set of objectives which constitute the primary reasons that children are in school. There is a tendency in human activity to choose those things which people find pleasurable and to find pleasurable those things in which they show either competence or ability to become competent or on occasions where they can set aside competence as a factor. Individuals tend to choose the things in the natural environment in which they can be successful. If you watch children in the preschool years, you will observe that they do things at which they are successful. If they fail at some activity, they either work to master it or they choose not to engage in it. When the child comes to school, the situation is fundamentally changed. For many children, the activities of school are not rewarding. They experience difficulty gaining competence, but they are still required to engage in the activity. The child who says, "I don't want to work on math because I am not good at it," is simply following the natural desire to do that which is satisfying. The rules which he meets in school are just the opposite. If he is not good at something, he must spend more time at that activity! If the child can see step-by-step success, the activity can become satisfying, but, if he experiences no satisfaction, asking him to continue the activity is like asking him to bang his head against the wall.

One of the major tasks in self-concept development is the acquisition of a system for dealing with incompetencies and failures. The system for dealing with failure or the development of such a system takes on prime importance when the child goes to school. The concept of "learner" involves the idea of moving toward greater competencies, but it also involves the idea of being incompetent at any point along the way. With the increased possibility of competency in school, the child is faced with the increased possibility of feelings of incompetence.

The possibility of increased feelings of incompetence is most prevalent for those pupils who have difficulty mastering the tasks required in school. These tasks can be intellectual or they can be the behavioral task of adjusting to the restrictive and rather passive behavior patterns required in most school situations. The intellectual concerns take on greater significance than they did before school because they predominate in school. When discussing self-concept, it must be assumed that the intellectual activities of school are extremely important. It is these activities which society has determined to be the major reason for the existence of schools. The importance of intellectual mastery is conveyed to the child by much of what society does. If the intellectual concerns are ignored in an attempt to deal with behavior or emotional difficulties, the problems are only compounded. Children know that they are supposed to be learning something in school, and, if the school neglects this learning while attempting to deal with other problems, the child frequently interprets this as a giving up on him. This perception increases the guilt and feelings of failure which characterize children with low self-images. For these reasons, many school personnel who have the primary task of counseling children feel that such counseling must include academic remediation if the behavior counseling is to be successful.

Boys seem to face greater difficulties than girls in entering the school situation. These difficulties for boys can be attributed to a number of causes. First of all, school is seen as a female place. In one study of sex designation of ordinary articles, it was found that almost all school-related objects are regarded by children as being "female" things (Kellogg, 1969). Why chalk, blackboards, chairs, desks, books, etc., are regarded as female is questionable but the findings suggest strongly that the boys operate in an environment which they perceive as being better suited for girls. Part of the

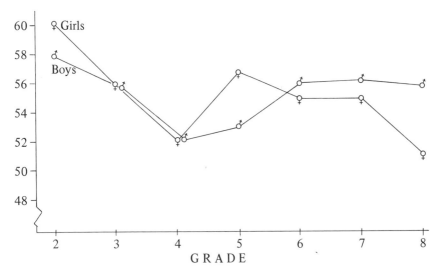

Figure 1. Self-Concept Scores across Grades 2 through 8 for Boys and Girls.

difficulty of school for boys is probably due to the slower developmental rate for boys as a group in comparison to girls as a group. Although this difference in developmental rate is most clearly characterized by the earlier onset of puberty for girls, it is a trend which runs through the developmental years.

Whatever the reasons, it is known that girls (as compared to boys) excel in a wide range of school-related skills (Ames & Ilg, 1964; Powell, O'Connor, & Parsley, 1964). The majority of children with behavior and discipline problems are boys (Moore, 1966). This fact suggests that the problem of handling failure while maintaining a positive self-image is more difficult for boys.

The roles of the school in self-concept development and of the teacher as the main agent of the school are crucial. There is some evidence, however, that the schools do not meet the problem of enhancing self-concept. As a group, elementary school children have difficulty maintaining positive self-concepts after they enter the school situation (Stanwyck, 1972).

Figure 1 shows the steady downward trend of self-concept as the child meets the pressures of the early school years. The sample on which these scores are based is from a suburban, middle-class, relatively new school with an excellent staff. One implication of this finding is that school by its very nature has a detrimental effect on the self-image of children. But it is encouraging that children as a group tend to develop ways of handling the school situation. Beginning at the fifth grade, they begin to become more positive in their self-concept. On the other hand, it is discouraging to look at the children who have the lowest self-concept scores and find that they do not show this upward surge at the fourth and fifth grade level but continue to have relatively negative self-concepts.

One conclusion that can be drawn from these data is that those students who enter school with a positive self-concept and have mechanisms for maintaining this self-concept are also able to adjust to school even though they may have some difficulty. For the child who does not have these mechanisms, the school situation only compounds his problems and increases the negative load which he must try to handle. Consequently, the pressures of school are likely to adversely affect those pupils who are already most hindered.

The sequence of changes through a child's school years illustrates the statement by McCandless at the beginning of this chapter: "Parents set the stage, but the play is acted out with peers, teachers, and bosses." For many teachers, the job is to see that the play is acted out so that the actors are not destroyed. For others, the job is to see that even though the actors are not prepared for the play, they begin to develop constructive ways of handling all of life by learning self-enhancing ways of dealing with the difficult task of school.

What the Teacher Can Do

The teacher who wants to help children handle the pressures of school in a manner which takes into account self-concept needs a set of principles on which to base his actions. In the remainder of this chapter, the Five Keys to Better Self-Concept will illustrate such a set of principles.

The Five Keys to Better Self-Concept were developed on two bases. First of all, they were developed by examining the literature of self-concept. An attempt was made to explain literature with the proposition that children develop a system of self-referent praise as a means of maintaining a positive self-concept. It was also postulated that, when this system is not developed, the child will not be able to maintain a positive self-concept when he faces everyday experience. Approaching self-concept enhancement in this manner has the advantage that it concentrates on a learning activity. Although most teachers may be aware of feelings and may be able to recognize internal perceptions, most teachers are not trained to deal with these areas of human experience. Teachers are trained to deal with learning problems. To approach self-concept from a learning model is to treat self-concept in a manner suited to teacher skills.

Secondly, the Five Keys to Better Self-Concept were developed by working with groups of teachers in teacher-training workshops. It was found that training teachers in this approach to self-concept enhancement resulted in more positive self-concept scores for their pupils, less anxiety, and fewer failure experiences (Felker, Stanwyck, & Kay, 1973).

The fact that this is an *action* program must be emphasized. It involves helping the child in specific ways to build up his self-concept. It is intended to help the child develop and maintain a positive self-concept.

Five Keys to Better Self-Concept are:

1. Adults, praise yourselves.
2. Help children to evaluate realistically.
3. Teach children to set reasonable goals.
4. Teach children to praise themselves.
5. Teach children to praise others.

Key I: Adults, Praise Yourselves

Try to think of the last time you did something that you felt you had done well. How would you describe the feelings which you had about the situation? Most people might characterize the feeling as good, or proud, or satisfied, or as some other similar adjective. Now try to think, did you say anything to anyone else about how you felt and about the fact that you had done a good job of which you were proud? The answer to that in most situations is no. Unless you are in a situation where you have a highly personal relationship, such as between a husband and wife, close friends, etc., you probably do not go around expressing self-satisfaction and self-compliments. Now think again, when you had these feelings of satisfaction and accomplishment, did you say anything quietly to yourself? You may have difficulty remembering what you say to yourself since inner speech tends to become automatic.

The next time you find that you are "talking to yourself," think about what you are saying. Probably, you will find that you have a running stream of inner language comprised of two primary types.

One type will be directions. You will find yourself telling yourself what to do in a specific situation. These directions allow you to work out problems without actually going through the manipulations. People think and internally talk through what they are to do in a situation, and this gives them a "cognitive" trial-and-error run at the problem.

In addition to the direction-giving role of inner language, you will find that you have a stream of reinforcing or suppressing language. You tell yourself that you are doing well or that you have done poorly. You point out successes and reprimand yourself for failures. This language keeps you going at those things that are successful and that you want to continue. Internal language also helps you eliminate those behaviors which are inappropriate. Self-control of behavior is a powerful method for changing and modifying behavior.

One of the important decisions for teachers is determining whether this internal use of language by the teacher is the best use of self-praise and self-direction as a teaching tool. Children learn much from models and imitation. Teachers use imitation frequently in the classroom. For example, the teacher works a problem to show the children how to do it and then the children imitate by performing or doing the same problem. The teacher says, "Let's walk through the halls quietly to the playground," and then leads the way and emphasizes the quietness by his actions. The gym teacher shows the pupils how to hold the ball to serve it in volleyball. In numerous ways, the normal classroom situation involves imitation as a teaching method.

Imagine for a moment a teacher who stands up and says, "This is the way to work the problem." She then stands for a few seconds and says, "Now do you all see?" But no one has seen anything because the teacher worked the problem in her head. The teacher may want the children eventually to work simple problems in their heads, and the problems may be simple enough for the teacher to work accurately in her head, but, when she is teaching the skill and during the time when the skill is being learned, something has to be externalized. If children are to learn from a model, they must see the model doing the skill to be learned. They cannot imitate an internal, cognitive function. In order to teach self-referent praise and reinforcement, the teacher must reinforce and praise herself vocally in front of the pupils. But this is a difficult task.

A friend of mine who teaches a course in self-concept development for high school pupils gave an assignment dealing with self-praise. Each member of the class was to say, "I'm a worthwhile person," to a parent, a peer, and another adult. They were to note particularly the response that they received from the various persons to whom they said, "I'm a worthwhile person." The responses ranged all the way from "What are you, some kind of a weirdo!" to mild rebuke, to no response, to mild reinforcement (such as "Everybody has a measure of worth") to a genuine positive reinforcement of "You sure are, Johnny." Among all the responses, there were many more on the negative than on the positive side. The only really positive response was made by a peer. The adults in the situation almost universally indicated that a statement of self-worth was inappropriate. It is difficult to determine whether people think it is actually inappropriate to think that one is a worthwhile person or whether they are saying that it is alright to think it but it is inappropriate to say it.

Like other adults, most teachers have adopted the idea that it is not modest to say nice things about oneself. They would feel uncomfortable going around saying nice things about themselves to other adults. In the school teaching situation, there are many things teachers do for and in front of the children which they would not do for or in front of adults. One doesn't say to a group of adults entering a building, "Now, let's make a special effort to be quiet, since it is not considerate to make noise that will disturb other people." An adult assumes that other adults have learned appropriate behavior. Assuming that a group of adults will act in an inconsiderate manner is insulting to the adults. Teachers don't assume that children have learned all appropriate behaviors since children are still in the learning stage. In a different culture where different behaviors were appropriate, it would not be out of order to instruct adults who were not acquainted with the behavior norms of that culture. Children are also learning to use self-referent positive language. The children are still in the learning state, and they need models. The problem of helping children to internalize this skill is one which comes after there is clear evidence that the child has developed the mechanisms and skills to reinforce himself. A teacher cannot teach children to work problems in their heads until he has some evidence that they can work the problems on paper. Similarly, teachers cannot teach internal use of language until they have some evidence that the child can use self-referent language overtly.

Another problem which tends to inhibit teachers from adopting the practice of openly praising themselves in front of children is the fear that they could become immodest and that pride could get the better of them. Someone remarked that if a person hugs himself once, he might find that it feels so good that he gets overenthusiastic and hugs himself to death. There are two factors which make this outcome unlikely. One is that there is constant pressure from the environment that operates against too much self-praise.

For example, our family purchased an old house which we remodeled. I enclosed the back porch, and, since I had never done anything like that before, I felt proud of the job that I had done constructing a door frame and installing the door. I was formulating some of my ideas on self-referent praise at that time, and I decided to try out some of the ideas. When my high school age daughter came home, I said, "Let me show you what a terrific job I did on this door!" I then took her out and showed her the door and explained some of the problems I had encountered and how I had solved them. She went into her room. Then my junior high school age daughter came home, and I repeated the process. She went in to talk with her older sister, and, while they were talking, my grade school age daughter came home. As I said, "Let me show you something," I heard one of my other daughters say, "If he doesn't get off that door kick, I think I will urp!" Children and adults will bring us back to reality if they find that we are overemphasizing.

The second factor which prevents teachers from overpraising themselves is that they have been trained not to self-praise at all. Adults have a built-in bias against self-praise, because as children they were taught by adults who had been taught that self-praise is immodest.

The crucial factor in approaching self-praise is to regard it as a learning and teaching opportunity. You may not feel comfortable when someone says something negative when you compliment yourself. Many teachers have found that if they say something like "I like the bulletin board I did" and a child says, "I don't," an opportunity is presented to teach the child that everyone has the right to like different things.

But how can you start to praise yourself and what should you praise? Look at some general guidelines which teachers who have tried this approach to self-concept development and enhancement have found helpful in applying this key to their classroom activities.

Begin praising yourself by expressing praise and satisfaction in areas where objective criteria are absent. It is easy for the inter-actions to become bogged down in an argument about whether the thing you have done or the product you have made is in fact "good." Although it will be necessary to look at the type of evaluation you have made, the object of this key is not to develop objective criteria of self-evaluation but to develop an openness for expressing self-praise and satisfaction. You might express how you feel about something you have done or made, such as "I really felt good when I looked at the bulletin board that I put up!" If someone in the class responds with something like "I don't think it is so great," it is then appropriate to say, "I didn't say it was great, but things don't have to be perfect for us to feel good about them." In this interaction, you are keeping the aim of the teaching centered around giving self-referent reinforcements and relating this to self-feelings. This aim relates to the second guideline.

Regard your use of self-reinforcement and positive self-referent language as a teaching opportunity and activity. One of the difficulties which adults have in applying Key One: Adults, Praise Yourselves is that they frequently get their own self-image so involved in the teaching activity that they forget that the primary purpose is to teach the children. Teachers have said that using the Five Keys has helped them to see themselves in a more positive manner, and this is a desirable consequence. But the *primary* purpose of applying the Five Keys is to help the children develop more positive self-concepts.

If you look at your self-praise as a teaching technique, the interactions which take place can be viewed not as a threat to your own self-concept but as an opportunity to help the child develop his self-concept. In this context, negative comments on your work become a learning problem and opportunity. The problem is "How to teach the child to be more positive with other people as a means of being more positive with himself?" Or the problem could be viewed as "How to teach the child that self-praise should be reinforced?" In both of these examples, notice that the emphasis is on teaching the child something. This approach has different consequences for the teacher than an approach which looks at self-praise as an end in itself. If it is an end in itself, the problem becomes "How do I receive reinforcements which confirm my positive statements?" Since the children have not yet been taught to give positive reinforcements for self-praise, such reinforcements are likely to be absent and hence the teacher will look at the interactions as a failure. The process of minimizing threats to the self-concept is important and is one of the reasons for the next guideline.

Begin self-praise by praising your work and then move to praising personal qualities. It is much more threatening to have someone dispute the image that you have of yourself as a person than it is to have someone dispute the evaluation that you have of your work.

This is partly because the meanings that individuals have attached to themselves, such as "good," "honest," "kind," etc., are an accumulation of a number of specific behavioral instances. To say that a person is a "good worker" carries more than the statement "This is a good piece of work which you have produced." Although both of these statements are important, the one (good worker) is perhaps more central to the self-concept than the other.

This same approach often occurs in the tendency that many parents and other adults have to generalize negative behaviors. Frequently, parents say, "Joey, you spilled your milk *again*! You are *always* spilling your milk!" It may be true that Joey has spilled his milk frequently, but the whole load of what he has done in the past is too much for him to handle during the pressure of trying to deal with milk running into his lap. A simple "You spilled your milk" would be sufficient for the moment, and a discussion later about his difficulties with spilled milk could help him to see what is happening. As a general rule, it is better to make negative instances very specific and not to let them turn into indications of the general character of the individual. On the other hand, positive instances should also be made specific, but then they should be allowed to generalize into a concept of self. Ginott (1965) has some interesting observations on types of appropriate praise.

When you are using self-praise, it is advantageous to begin with things which are not highly personal so that the possible attacks on your self-concept will be minimized. One way that threats are reduced is to deal with accomplishments rather than personal qualities. It is important, however, to move at some point into the more personal qualities so that the children begin to see that the model in the situation is allowed to say nice things about himself and not only about what he makes or does.

The fourth guideline deals more directly with the problem of showing children what is going on. When applying Key One, it is helpful to tell your class what you are doing. Some teachers have found that direct teaching in this area is useful. You can make a bulletin board on which you display the Five Keys to Better Self-Concept, or you can have a teaching lesson on self-concept and on how what people do affects younger children who watch them. You then can look at the children in your class as models for younger siblings and peers. You might have a poster or a set of posters on which the Five Keys are written. You could have an "I'm O.K. day," during which everyone is supposed to say something nice about themselves or write a story about the thing they did which they felt best about. You could then write your own story and read it to the class as an example.

All of these suggestions would have applications to each of the Five Keys, but many teachers have found that the reactions of children to Key One are the most unusual. Children are not accustomed to hearing teachers praise themselves, and they really don't know how to act in the new situation. Explaining to pupils what is going on and discussing reactions and how to respond to people when they say something nice to themselves is one way of learning. Another way to let the children know what is going on is to use responses to self-praise as an opportunity to explain to them what you are doing. You could even say something like "You got a funny look on your face when I said, 'I like the bulletin board.' Do you know why I said that?" You then could go on to tell the children that you want them to know that it is alright to say nice things when they feel good about what they have done and that one of the joys of life is to share our good feelings with each other and to tell ourselves about it.

The fifth guideline for using Key One affects most of the previous guidelines. Practice self-praise internally. For most of you, praising yourself is a new activity. It is not something that will come easily, but it is something that will produce dividends. One technique for feeling more comfortable with a new activity is to practice it. You can practice self-praise in a sheltered situation such as your family. Explain to your family that you are starting something new at school; then explain what it is, and tell them you want to try it out at home. Another sheltered way of practicing is simply to note places where self-praise might have been appropriate and then play "What I should have said" with yourself. Think about what was said and force yourself to say the self-praise out loud. One of the reasons self-referent praise is so difficult is that the words simply don't sound natural. If you force yourself to say positive things out loud, you get accustomed to hearing yourself say such things, and they will not sound nearly so strange when you do say them in a group.

With the preceding guidelines in mind, look at some classroom situations that lend themselves to praise.[1] The general situations in which each of the Five Keys can be applied are task situations, personal situations, and environmental situations. The teacher has

[1]The following rationale and outline are adapted from *Self-Concept Observation Record* which was developed as a part of Grant MH19384 from the National Institute of Mental Health, United States Department of Health, Education and Welfare to the author of this text.

many activities or tasks which are a part of his work, and the teacher, when given an opportunity, can express approval or pleasure in doing a good job. In the personal area, the teacher, when given an opportunity, can express approval or pleasure about physical self, appearance, mental condition, or some other personal characteristic. In the environmental category, the teacher, when given an opportunity, can express approval or pleasure in contributing to a positive or productive classroom atmosphere or to general conditions of life.

You can readily see that the teacher also could teach children to praise themselves in these same areas or to praise each other so that these categories are applicable to others of the Five Keys. Within each of these categories, the teacher can express praise and satisfaction for a number of different reasons. Although the number of reasons for praise is extensive, in classroom observations it has been found that most can be classified under the following five reasons for praise:

1. Praise for mental attitudes or conditions—feelings and ideas.
2. Praise for *choice* of materials.
3. Praise for result achieved.
4. Praise for methods used in achieving an end result.
5. Praise for *reactions* to end results.

Each of these reasons for praise can stimulate a broad range of adjectives which will express praise. In fact, one teacher had her class construct a list of adjectives which they interpreted as meaning "good." It included expressions such as tough, groovy, fantabulous, starry, and unlimited. Each school and age group might have a list of adjectives which they use to express praise, and it is sometimes a difficult task for the teacher to master the phrases used by children. For example, I have difficulty calling something "tough" as a compliment. An occasional use of some of the more current praise words is useful because it attracts the attention of the pupils. Some of the more traditional words to express praise for mental attitudes or conditions could be right, bright, good, and brilliant. The choice of materials could be effective, reliable, modern, or attractive. Good, looks good, correct, super, and likable can describe a result or a product. A method can be quick, organized, efficient, or enjoyable. Reactions can be praised as earned, deserved, or the result of hard work. One of the reasons these adjectives are mentioned is that it is common to find teachers using a word such as "good" to describe all positive behaviors and outcomes in the class. The word takes on such a generalized connotation that is loses its power as a praise word for individual effort and behavior. You might make a chart of adjectives. From the present paragraph, you would have over 20 praise words. Keep track of how many times you use them to give evaluative feedback and praise to yourself and to others in the environment. There are some extremely good (!) words which are little used in the vocabulary of self- and other-praise words.

The process of self-referent positive language or self-praise is an unusual and frequently new process, and there is much in American society that works against its use. But if children are going to learn the skills which will enhance and maintain a positive self-image, teachers must look at this area from the standpoint of a learning situation. It is useful to keep in mind that the ultimate goal is internalized reinforcement that allows the child to be an independent, self-motivated individual with a positive self-concept (Felker & Stanwyck, 1973). Self-praise by adults in the presence of children is one step in the learning process which will achieve a goal. Since the practice of self-praise is new and may cause some unusual reactions, some workable guidelines have been established. Also some of the classroom situations in which self-praise is most appropriate have been outlined. Before going on to Key Two, it should be pointed out that a commitment to Key One on the part of teachers provides the groundwork for the other Keys. If as a teacher you are not willing to commit yourself to being a model, it is questionable whether you will commit yourself to teaching children something which you yourself are not willing to do.

The best way to approach the Five Keys is to go before reading further and try Key One. Note the reactions and the feelings which you have while praising yourself. Come back and reread this section on Key One. You may find that some of the questions raised by your experience are answered and that you did not notice the answers the first time you read the section. Practice some of the suggestions and then try the process again. Afterward, you will be ready to start applying the remainder of the Five Keys.

One final guideline: Don't expect immediate and dramatic changes in yourself or in your pupils. Self-concept is an unusually stable variable, because it is one of the primary mechanisms that humans use to interpret what happens to them. Changes are going to be relatively difficult and slow; in fact, changes are likely to be more swift for your students than for you. The older you are, the more experience you have that has determined how you will look at yourself and how you will look at the world. Self-concept not only is influenced by what is done and what happens to individuals as they develop, it is an active force in determining the force that these experiences have upon the individual. The view that an individual has developed gives him a set of expectations and a predisposition to interpret events in a particular way. If one expects to be cheated in a store, he is likely to interpret any behavior by the store personnel as confirmation of his expectation to be cheated. The individual who sees himself as a failure is likely to interpret any difficulties as confirmation of the fact that he is a failure. The person who sees himself or herself as unlovely is likely to interpret many happenings as evidence that he is, in fact, unlovely. In this sense, the self-concept moves from being a product to being a producer. But the self-concept also influences the interpretation which individuals give to the past. It is often said that you cannot change the past—you just have to live with it. Although it is true that you cannot change what happened in the past, you can change your impressions and interpretation of its meaning.

Each individual reinterprets the past in light of the present. How often have you changed your opinion of the past on the basis of the present? I recently talked with a young man in the army who said, "Being in the army really made me see how good a thing it was that my folks harangued me into finishing high school." His present experiences had changed his perception of what had gone on in his last years of high school.

The fact that self-concept helps individuals give meaning to the past, the present, and the future means that the self-concept influences their total experiences. The self-concept helps them make sense out of what is going on around them. But this mechanism also means that the self-concept is relatively difficult to change since it operates as the filter through which other experiences are interpreted. Small goals should be set for changes and small but significant goals for the behavior of pupils. The goals should be set in relation to the particular thing you are trying to accomplish such as "praising myself at least once today," rather than some wider outcome such as "being a person who is self-praising."

The process of how well you are doing is also crucial to a better self-concept for children and is important in Key Two.

Key Two: Help Children Evaluate Realistically

A number of years ago, Jersild (1963) pointed out that one of the general characteristics of individuals with negative self-concepts is that they make unrealistically high demands upon themselves. People with low self-esteem tend to judge themselves on the basis of unattainable goals of perfection. In the analysis of self-concept using a model involving self-referent praise, it is easy to see that realistic evaluations play a central role in the use of self-referent positive language as a mechanism for maintaining a positive self-concept. If the individual is consistently evaluating himself against some unrealistic benchmark, he is bound to perceive that most of his efforts are failures. If he perceives that his efforts are failures, self-reinforcement, and self-referent praise are inappropriate, because one doesn't want to build up or reinforce failure behavior. Self-reinforcement is only appropriate following success or at least progress toward success. If a person is judging himself from some sort of unrealistic base, he probably will not have a positive self-concept.

Helping children evaluate themselves realistically is an important factor often ignored in many achievement situations. Children do not naturally develop a basis for realistic evaluation and self-rewards. Instead, they tend to be overly harsh in their evaluations and they tend to give themselves fewer rewards than adults would deem appropriate in the same situation (Bandura & Perloff, 1967). It has been shown, however, that children with various backgrounds can become more accurate and realistic in their self-evaluations (Barrett, 1968; Werblo & Torrance, 1966).

There are two characteristics which evaluations must entail if they are to contribute to the maintenance of a positive self-concept. One characteristic is accuracy, and the other characteristic is realism. Children have false negative evaluations basically for two reasons: One reason can be inaccuracy in evaluating what in fact has been done. This is typical of the child who looks at his test paper and says, "I know I failed," when in fact he has a very high score. The second type of false negative evaluation occurs when the child accurately appraises what has been done but gives an unrealistic connotation to it. The child may accurately estimate that his grade point average will be 5.9 out of a possible 6.0. If he then interprets this as a failure because he did not have a perfect record or because someone else did have a perfect record, he is giving himself a false negative evaluation. It is not uncommon for salutatorians to feel that they have failed because they did not outrank the valedictorian. Rather than looking with pride on the fact that they have an outstanding record which ranked them second in the graduating class, they give a negative connotation to a basically accurate evaluation. This type of evaluation is accurate, but it lacks realism. Notice that both types of image-shattering "failures" are different and have different consequences than the situation where an individual actually does fail a task. True failure also should be based on an accurate assessment and realistic evaluation. When you are dealing with true failure, look at it from the standpoint of learning. Improvement and learning extend the possibility of turning the experience of true failure into one which will build up the individual's self-concept. With inaccurate assessment and unrealistic evaluation, however, it is not a problem of learning and gaining skill; it is a problem of false interpretation of what has been done. If the individual bases his evaluations on perfection, anything short of perfect performance will be evaluated as failure.

Failure is an experience which must be faced by children, but the unrealistic evaluations that many children are taught only compound the problems of real failure. Unrealistic evaluations lead to generalizing failure to all experiences. The child begins to anticipate failure and to interpret all experiences as failure experiences.

The purpose of Key Two is not to have children completely avoid negative evaluations. Some realistic evaluations may be negative, but a negative evaluation which is realistic provides a basis for change that will allow positive performance and therefore positive evaluation. When an evaluation is unrealistic, a change in performance or learning is not likely to influence substantially the evaluation.

The essence of Key Two is in the word *realistic*. What is a realistic evaluation? One characteristic already pointed out is that realism is not based on perfection as the basis of evaluation. Even in religious literature, the evaluations of mankind on the basis of a perfect standard are accompanied by the concept of grace. Jesus, for example, said, "Be ye therefore perfect, even as your Father which is in heaven is perfect" (Matt. 5:48). But this requirement of perfection is accompanied by the concepts of grace and substitutionary perfection when the perfection which is lacking in man is provided by grace from the supernatural father. The requirements of perfection in religion are of a different nature than the requirements of perfection which often operate in human interactions. Children who are learning are not perfect and will never reach perfection. Adults who require that their performance be perfect before it is acceptable to themselves are likely to be in a constant state of perceived failure. Adults who require perfection from other adults and children are requiring more than is realistic or kind.

The second characteristic of realistic evaluation is that the evaluation be based on *past* performance. In other words, present evaluations should be in relation to past accomplishments of the *individual*. Much evaluation in school systems is based on comparing the performance of an individual child to the general performance of a group of children. For example, the principal of a school which my children attended said at a PTA meeting, "The standardized scores of our children averaged at the 73rd percentile on national norms." He paused and then said, "But you must keep in mind that average in our school is very much above average." The whole concept of trying to decide what average work is means that the child's performance is judged on the basis of where his performance would place him in the group of children. If it is a group that is performing at a high level, the child who is at the bottom of the group many times feels as though he is failing when, in fact, the child's actual level of performance may be very satisfactory if judged on some other basis than the performance of the total group in which he happens to find himself. For performance standards to be realistic, they must take into account where the child has started and whether his behavior and performance is realistic in relation to his past performance.

Judging children on other than group norms is an extremely difficult concept to practice in a typical school system. Teachers and parents are so used to the usual A through F grading system that even children in the very early grades find themselves bound to the system. My family once lived in a school district where the grading system was going to be revamped. The grades were going to be 1-exceptional progress; 2-above average progress; 3-reasonable progress; 4-better progress can be achieved. The first report card date came and I asked my second grade son, "How did you do on your report card?" His reply was "Two Bs, and three Cs." I said, "I thought that they quit giving grades on the cards." To which he replied, "Oh, they did. But everybody knows that a 1 is the same as an A and a 2 is the same thing as a B." Breaking the system is difficult, but the teacher needs techniques whereby he can give reinforcements and, if necessary, give grades on the basis of evaluation of the child as compared with his own past performance.

Realistic evaluation also must be specific. Teachers tend to give total grades and reinforcements rather than evaluations of specific, small areas of good and poor performance. It is interesting that in a study of boys' reactions to failure it was found that boys with positive self-concepts have learned to deal with failure partly by connecting failure statements with success statements. They are likely to greet a failure with statements such as, "Sometimes I succeed and sometimes I fail" or "Usually I do things correctly."

However, boys with negative self-concepts are likely to greet failure with a statement that generalizes the failure; for example, "I can never do anything right," or "I always fail" (Felker, 1972). One way to maintain a positive self-concept in the face of failure is to defend oneself against the failure's interpretation as usual or expected behavior. A teacher can approach the failure experiences of pupils in the same way by using statements such as "You blew it, but you will do better next time" or "You only got two right, how unlike you" or "You were wrong this time, but you will probably be right the next time" or "You got the last two items right, but you really bombed the first part of the test" or "The total paper was inadequate, but I think you have a good enough idea to warrant rewriting it" or "Your paper was a little thin on ideas but I like this part—expand it." These are all statements which cushion failure with success, and there are numerous other statements that help connect failure with hope and help connect the present with reinforcing past performances.

One way of handling evaluations is to have the children keep track of performance. This can be done by having simple cards that serve as charts on which each child can chart his own performance. The card might look something like the one below.

The card can be taped to the child's desk and serve as a reminder of how he is doing in relation to how he has done in the immediate past. This approach has the added advantage of moving the evaluation to the child and away from the teacher.

It should be pointed out that, when you move toward having the child evaluate himself on the basis of his past performance, you are

| NAME _____ |
| No. Right: 1 2 3 4 5 6 7 8 9 10 |
| Quiz |
| V |
| IV |
| III |
| II |
| I |

giving up perfection as an appropriate standard, that you are giving up the practice of comparing children to each other, and that you are giving up percentage of correct answers as a measure of success. What you are adopting is a system based on the conviction that any improvement is good and that the way to greater success and adequate performance usually comes in small steps. Each of the small steps should be encouraged, and the child should be taught to look at improvement as a reason for self-praise and self-encouragement.

This process of self-evaluation is also vitally connected with the next key to a positive self-concept.

Key Three: Teach Children to Set Realistic Goals

The process of evaluation is connected with goal-setting in that the goal operates many times as the standard against which the individual evaluates himself. If the goals are unrealistic or unreasonable, the individual is in a sense adopting a standard of evaluation which is unrealistic. The two processes of goal-setting and evaluating could be handled as two parts of one process. Usually in the classroom setting, however, the two processes are separated during learning activities and, therefore, they will be considered separately.

The child comes into most learning environments with some goals already in his repertoire. Then he is faced with a learning task and performs. Next, he evaluates his performance on the basis of how well he achieved the goal he had set. This process provides the basis for the next goal and is ongoing and circular. It would be expected that individuals would set their goals in relation to what they have done in the past, but the literature on goal-setting indicates that this is not always the case (Kay, 1972). For example, it was found that individuals with negative self-concepts set their goals either unrealistically low or unrealistically high. In either situation, the outcome would be perceived as failure. If the goal is unrealistically low, the achievement of the goal is not an accomplishment. The individual can regard his performance as meeting the goal, but he can perceive also that the goal was set so low that anyone, "even me," could reach it. If the goal is set unreasonably high, a similar process of perceived failure will operate for the negative self-concept individual. In this case, he may regard the goal as appropriate and his performance as a failure.

This reasoning is based on the assumption and some empirical evidence that individuals will act in ways that are consistent with their present self-concept and will tend to maintain it (Lecky, 1951). This reasoning process shows clearly that goals can be used in the service of the self-concept. To approach goal-setting as only an influence on self-concept, rather than as a tool which the self-concept uses, is to ignore a potentially powerful idea. It was found, for example, that those who have positive self-concepts can use goals as a means of maintaining the present level of self-concept. Kay (1972) found that one group of positive self-concept boys were characterized by high goal-setting and tended to blame failure on forces outside themselves. Each boy could enhance or maintain his self-concept by perceiving that he could achieve much (high goal-setting) and still defend himself against the resulting non-accomplishment of the goal by denying that the lack of accomplishment was his doing. In other words, he could blame his failure on someone or something else in the environment.

Even though such mechanisms operate to defend and in some cases to maintain a positive self-concept, they are not preferred methods. Such mechanisms involve distortions of events in the environment. Blaming failure on someone else does not do anything toward solving the persistent problem of failure. Such means of handling failure cultivate the bias of not accepting responsibility for individual actions. Over a period of time, the externalization of responsibility is likely to develop the perception of powerlessness in the face of overwhelming forces. A perception of powerlessness is one of the characteristics of individuals with unusually negative self-concepts. Although denial of self-responsibility for failure may be a useful mechanism for boys to use in facing the aggravated rate of failure in early elementary school, it does not offer the long-term self-enhancement potential of reasonable goal-setting.

The process of realistic goal-setting is countered with some social pressure in the opposite direction. American society has adopted the principle that high goals are to be stated and maintained, even if the goals are not actually attainable. Statements such as "Aim high" or "You will never reach anything unless you aim high" are common. There may be a grain of truth in a statement of this type, but the wholesale acceptance of the necessity for high goals has produced unrealistic goal-setting in many children. A typical example is the interaction that takes place when a child comes into a schoolroom like this.

Teacher: Johnny, how many spelling words are you going to get right on your spelling today?

Johnny: I think I will get three out of ten right.
Teacher: Johnny, you will never make it in spelling unless you are willing to try harder than that!!

Johnny then takes the test and gets two correct (his average score for the school year on spelling tests). The scene switches to the next week as Johnny enters the classroom.

Teacher: Well, Johnny, you did not do too well on your spelling test last week. How many are you going to try to get correct today?
Johnny: I'm going to try to get them all right.
Teacher: That's the way to try, Johnny. It is better to try and fail than not to try at all.

From the standpoint of learning, it is questionable whether it is better to try and fail than not to have tried at all. It is certain that it is better to try and succeed than to try and fail. If teachers feel they must set goals high in order to motivate pupils, they are conditioned to unrealistic goals that will produce efforts which will be classified as failures.

The concept of realistic goal-setting dictates that the goals which the individual sets must have three characteristics: (1) they must be individual; (2) they must be made in relation to past performance; and (3) they must have both a goal and an end in view.

Frequently, the goals which children adopt are not ones which they have had an active part in setting. Their goals are ones which have been determined externally by the teacher, parent, or some other source. The process of individual goal-setting produces a number of benefits. One is that the individual experiences achievement of goals. In addition, he learns something about the type of goals to set, the process of setting them, and the process of attempting to reach them.

What goes into the process of setting goals? This is a question for which pupils many times receive few answers. But in spite of this, students constantly have goals toward which they are striving. Another side benefit is that individual and personal involvement in goal-setting requires a commitment to the goal. If the individual student has had no part in setting the goal, it is easy for him to lack commitment to it. An easy defense, if the goal is not reached, is that the "teacher expected too much" or "the goal was set too high" or "things were unreasonable" or "no one should be required to try to do so much." Each of these defense statements assumes that the requirements and the goals are external. When the individual has engaged in the goal-setting process himself, such defenses are more difficult. Rather than developing defenses to justify why he did not attain the goal, the pupil can use failure to meet the goal as an opportunity for further learning about how to set goals. The performance can be judged in relation to the goal. The process also can be turned around and he can decide whether or not there was something unrealistic about the goal. Should the goal have been set lower? How much lower would be reasonable? The pupil learns as he deals with these questions. With the help of the teacher, he can learn more about the elements of goal-setting.

The second characteristic which realistic goals must have is that they must be made in relation to past performance. Just as evaluation must be individual in the sense of making judgments in relation to what the individual has done in the past, goal-setting must be done in the same context. Most of the literature on goal-setting and levels of aspiration (the levels of performance to which an individual aspires on the next try) indicates that the most reasonable type of goal-setting occurs when the goal is *slightly* higher than previous performances (Kay, 1972). For many children, this may be at a level far below the eventual performance toward which they are striving or toward which the teacher is aiming. But the lower level is reasonable in the sense that it is attainable. Goals which are not attainable do not contribute to long-term performance. What is attainable today is largely dependent upon what was attained yesterday, last week, or last month. If goals are going to be realistic and individual, the goal-setter must take into account past levels of performance.

The third characteristic of realistic goal-setting is partially an application of the first two characteristics. In realistic goal-setting, there must be both an *end-goal* and an *end-in-view* or a *goal-in-view*. For example, a recent newspaper cartoon showed a caterpillar inching its way up a hill. It said, "I'm going from here to there." The next two frames showed the caterpillar huffing and puffing. In the last frame, the caterpillar said, "Could you come back later, it takes quite a while to get from here to there."

Frequently, teachers forget that learning progress is slow and comes in very, very small units. Even when they take this fact into account in the methods that they use to teach children, they often omit this factor when they help pupils set goals. However, children do not feel comfortable with low goals. Teachers who have worked on goal-setting techniques have reported that children, when asked how many times they will try to answer correctly, usually set goals which are high in relation to what they have been doing. The most appropriate response to overzealous goal-setting is one like "Good! Let's put that down as the goal that you are really aiming for. Now let's look at where you are now. Okay. Let's draw a line from here to there. Now, what is the first step you have to go through to get from here to there. Right! Now, let's make that your goal for today. Okay? And when you get to that step, then we will see what is the next step."

This kind of a teaching process is not difficult. The amazing thing to teachers is that it results in greater performance than that which is gained using unrealistic goal-setting. In one class in an inner-city school with children who were almost all performing at a low level, the teacher found that this approach was so successful that in the first week all of her pupils, except one, exceeded the goal-in-view.

Having short-range, attainable goals-in-view allows the child to see that he is dealing with something that is possible. It also allows self-reinforcement and increases opportunities for external reinforcement. If goals are set at an unattainable level, it is rather insincere to praise the child after performance. It is obvious to him and to the teacher that he has not done a "good job." But if the goals are small and attainable, the basis for frequent and sincere praise is present.

In applying Key Three, "Help children to set realistic goals," teachers have found that individual charts for the children to keep track of their goal-setting and performance are helpful. Such a card could be similar to the one on page 78, but it would include space for both goals and scores. Whatever the teacher designs as an aid for the children, the form should have on it the aspects of performance, a starting point, a final goal point, and an indication of the small steps in between.

The comments and activities of the teacher can also be aimed at helping the child see the connection between his present position or present performance, the goal which is to be achieved, the means of achieving that goal, and the intermediate goals that are involved in achieving the ultimate goal. Teachers often restrict goals to some type of grade, percentage, or number that deals with performance in academic areas. Children have goals in other areas, and these goals also can be used in teaching them how to set goals in a realistic manner. Other goals could have to do with sports, personal projects, money saving, behavior that is not academic, contests, and innumerable other areas.

Teaching children to set reasonable goals is a major step in the process of helping them to become more self-praising and to develop internal mechanisms for enhancing and maintaining a positive self-concept.

Key Four: Teach Children to Praise Themselves

There has been increasing emphasis in recent years on the powerful influence exerted by teachers through verbal statements. Whole programs for modifying the behavior of children have been developed and have been found effective for changing the particular behavior of a child (Poteet, 1973). Many of these programs are labeled behavioral modification and operate to modify the child's behavior through reinforcements by the teacher.

In addition to the moral and ethical questions associated with manipulating the behavior of pupils, there is evidence that humans react differently than animals because they control and direct their own behavior on internal bases (Felker, 1973). For example, some people reject high payoff activities when they perceive that they are not in control of the payoff (Rotter, 1966). It has also been pointed out that there is growing evidence that human behavior is extensively under self-reinforcement control (Bandura, 1971).

One of the assumptions behind the Five Keys is that human behavior should be largely self-controlled. Although the early learning of humans is dependent upon others, the results of early learning become internalized and begin to filter and direct the experience of the individual. The emphasis which is placed on the internal control and direction of the individual is one of the primary factors which distinguishes the present approach from behavioral modification. All of the activities in the Five Keys are designed to increase the individual's control of himself and not the control of the individual by an outside agent such as a teacher.

In the context of self-enhancement, the pupil must become his own evaluator and reinforcer. He must develop the habit and the skills necessary to give himself verbal praise when it is appropriate. The child can use other means of reinforcement, such as rewards (grades), physical comforts (jelly beans), rest (time away from work), or pleasure (fun activities), but these are all dependent upon some external circumstance or object. For example, the child cannot give himself a jelly bean when there are no jelly beans available. Verbal comments, on the other hand, are internal and are always available to the individual. Verbal rewards also can operate in a circular manner. Not only is the behavior in which the individual has engaged reinforced and more likely to occur again, but positive statements are reinforced by the successful behavior so that one becomes reinforcing of the other.

The practice of having the child give himself verbal praise also allows the teacher more freedom in that she no longer is the sole dispenser of reinforcements. It is impossible for the teacher to be aware of all behavior which is going on in the classroom. One informal observation study at the Institute for Child Study, University of Maryland, indicated that the teacher must make upwards of 350 decisions an hour when working with children in a classroom setting. Even with this tremendous decision load, there is much that is going on with individual children of which the teacher cannot be aware. In addition to the limitations on his time, range, and finite ability to pay attention to the stimuli in the school environment, there are pupil activities which by their nature are hidden from the teacher. For example, a pupil thinks to himself and comes up with a correct answer; he watches another pupil give the answer that he thought of at the same time. These and other activities are hidden from the teacher, and he therefore cannot reinforce them. He may say to one child "good," and, if another child is imitating him, it would be reinforcing to both children but this would cover only a small number of instances in comparison to everything that is going on among the pupils.

A system which frees the teacher and moves the responsibility and skill for reinforcing back to the individual pupil is desirable. It is not necessary, in fact it is impossible, for the teacher to reinforce everything that is desirable in a pupil. If the pupil has learned to give himself verbal praise, the reinforcement goes on without the teacher. Just as the jelly beans as an external reinforcer become superfluous, the teacher's verbal reinforcements become superfluous. The teacher in a sense works himself out of the job of the primary reinforcing agent in the classroom. This role is taken over by the individual pupil for himself, and the teacher is freed to help other students who have difficulty learning to be their own reinforcers or who start out with a negative, suppressing set of internal verbal communications.

The self-concept is basically internal. The self-concept is the internal perceptions and concepts which individuals have of themselves. Part of self-concept is the meaning that individuals attach to words that are self-words. The meaning which is attached to "me" is part of the concept, and it follows then that part of the task of developing and maintaining a positive self-concept is to develop a new set of verbal meanings to these self-properties.

Teaching the child to engage in self-praise is not only teaching him to reinforce his behavior, it is teaching him a new set of self-referent ideas. To say, "I did well on that," not only reinforces what it was that was done, it attaches to "I" the label "well-doer." It is this aspect of self-praise that is the most important for self-concept. People maintain their ideas, including the ideas which they have about themselves, with a system of words. A set of positive words and phrases which the child learns to apply to himself is a powerful mechanism for self-esteem.

The answer to the question "Should adults teach children to praise themselves?" is a solid "yes." But this answer raises a second question—"Why don't they?" There are a number of reasons why most adult-child teaching situations do not involve a teaching of self-praise. Some of the reasons are the same as those which operate to prohibit adults from praising themselves.

Most of these prohibitions center around two fears. One is the fear that the child will be taught to be immodest or that people will think him immodest. The distinction between an habitual behavior and a behavior that is a necessary step toward an ultimate goal has already been discussed. If the child (or the adult for that matter) is going to develop an internalized set of positive self-referent statements, it is necessary at some point that the teacher be assured that he has such a set of statements. The only way the teacher can be assured is to hear the statements, and then he can attend to the process of helping the child to say them to himself. It may help to perceive this set of statements as self-encouraging statements rather than as self-praising statements. This approach would alleviate some of the socially negative connotations which have been attached to self-praise.

The second set of fears results from the kinds of responses individuals have been taught to expect from other people. Many adults hesitate to praise themselves because they fear that they will have this praise challenged by someone in the environment. The challenge will usually be ego threatening and will challenge the positive view which they have of themselves. Children who praise themselves are under even greater ego threats than adults. They are surrounded by other kids in the classroom who may be waiting to pounce on them with negative statements in addition to a teacher who may tell them, "Don't be so proud! Quit bragging!"

The teacher is the only one in the classroom who can cultivate a climate in which self-encouragement and self-reinforcement are considered acceptable behavior. If the teacher is willing to put his "self" on the line and engage in self-encouragement in front of the children and to actively teach them methods of self-praise, it becomes acceptable behavior.

Some teachers have found it successful and comparatively non-threatening to develop a system of group praise and to move later to individual self-praise. This can be done by helping the class as a unit or as small groups within the class to openly praise themselves. Statements such as "We did a good job in our reading group today, didn't we?" encourage group praise. One teacher even created class cheers and ended each day with "Who can do it, class?" The class would reply by shouting, "Room 54 can do it!" This became the cry of the class every time there was a call for volunteers to do anything in the school.

The teacher felt that this was a good way of building class pride and consequently building the pride of each member. It was also a relatively nonthreatening way to get the class accustomed to making praise statements. From group praise, the teacher moved without great difficulty into individual self-praise and self-encouragement.

A skillful use of question-asking is one of the tools for teaching children self-praise. When the teacher asks a question, he is usually trying to elicit a response from the students. The emphasis on the Five Keys to Better Self-Concept is on the pupil's response to himself. It has been found in classroom observations that teachers can use skillful question-asking as a means of eliciting self-encouragement, self-evaluation, and goal-setting. When the child responds, the teacher can reinforce that response or elicit the reinforcement from the pupil with a question such as "Don't you think you did well on that?" The pupil's response can then receive a praise statement such as "I think you did a tremendous job, too. You really should give yourself a pat on the back." When the children are accustomed to giving self-referent verbal reinforcement, the teacher can ask, "What do you think you should say to yourself?" The normal reply will be "I don't know." Follow this with "What do I say to you when I think you did a good job?" Then, "Well, since you think you did a good job, why don't you say the same thing to yourself?" Questions call for the child to take part in the process, and they help him make the applications of praise.

Key Five: Teach Children to Praise Others

An interesting finding is that self-praise and praise of others are positively related (Coons & McEachern, 1967). The tendency is to assume that, when people are reinforcing of themselves, they will be nonreinforcing to others, but the opposite is true. It appears that learning to praise is a general skill which is applied to similar situations and is increasingly applied to self and others. Key Five and Key Four are related. Increasing one is likely to increase the activity in the other. The increase comes about in two ways. One way is that each of the individuals in the situation learns the skill of praise giving. Each is then more likely to apply praise in both self and other situations. The second way is that each individual becomes a reinforcer for the other individuals. As a result, he is more likely to meet with positive responses which will increase his praising behavior.

My wife teaches a Sunday school class of four-year-olds. Recently, one boy who was not interested in joining anything which the class was doing said, "This story is stupid!" My wife ignored him for a little while until he said, "That picture is stupid!" My wife replied, "Oh? I think it's a pretty picture!" The boy then said, "This class is stupid!" My wife decided that some learning should take place and said, "The class is not stupid and I don't think that you really think it is stupid. You are mad about something and so you are saying the class is stupid. When you say that things are stupid, people don't like it and they don't say anything nice back to you. Why don't you say that you like something and see how nice it makes you feel and how nice it feels when people smile at you?" The boy sat for a while, and, when the teacher was not paying close attention to him, he looked at the little boy next to him and said, "I like you." The little boy broke out in a big smile and said, "I like you too!" The class was much better the rest of the hour.

Praising others brings praise and reinforcement in return. People like to be reinforced and they respond in pleasant ways. Many of the difficulties which were noted in connection with adults praising themselves and teaching children to praise themselves apply to this key also. Praise in all of its forms, whether directed to self or to others, is pleasant and reinforcing, but it is also threatening. When one says to oneself, "I'm okay," there is always the possibility that someone will say, "No, you are not." When one says, "I like you!" the probabilities are in his favor that he will get a positive response. There is always a chance, however, that he will receive instead "I hate you!" The negative responses are usually so unpleasant that the thought of receiving one keeps people from attempting praise of self and others.

The threatening aspects of praise mean that the teacher has a twofold job using Key Five. He must teach children how to give praise to others, and he must teach children how to receive praise from others. Children normally have to learn how to receive praise, just as they have to learn how to give praise. The two processes can be taught simultaneously, particularly if giving praise back is emphasized as one way of receiving praise.

Teachers who have tried the Five Keys in classroom settings have found that cultivating open sharing time has been effective. Teachers are used to sharing time in the sense of sharing objects, and some have used the same idea to help children share personal and emotional things. For example, "Today we are going to share with each other the most scary thing that ever happened to us" or "Today we are going to share with each other the nicest thing that ever happened to us" or "Today we are going to share the nicest thing that a person has ever done for us." This sharing allows the children to see that each child and adult is an individual and that each has emotions, desires, and experiences.

Another requirement is that children receive some help helping other children. It has been found that peer tutors are extremely effective helpers for other children (Felker, Stanwyck, & Kay, 1973). But other children need training in how to help another pupil. They need specific training in when to give praise and what to do when a child fails. The teacher can look at it as a short course in the Five Keys. One reason they need training is that most children have learned ineffective behavior from adults. Adults and many teachers have fallen into the habit of always pointing out mistakes and incorrect behavior and generally ignoring good behavior. If children are playing gently at home, parents tend to leave them alone. But if the kids start climbing or walking on the sofa, one of the parents soon pays some attention to them. If children are working quietly by themselves, the teacher leaves them alone, but, if the group gets rowdy, the teacher steps in. This is appropriate teacher behavior *after* the children have developed an effective system of self-reinforcement and self-praise. Then, the children have self-referent praise operating so that when they are doing well they are not dependent upon outside sources of praise. Before the child has formulated completely his system of praise, ignoring him when he is doing well and paying attention to him when he is doing poorly is teaching him that it is appropriate to self-ignore good behavior and to self-rebuke poor performance. If he copies the teacher and does this, he is learning that when he does well he is not supposed to say anything to himself and when he does poorly he is supposed to say something negative to himself. He will not have a system of self-referent encouragement and praise but will have a system of self-rebuke.

It is imperative that children learn how to praise others by being taught what to ignore, how to handle failure situations, and when to reinforce. This also operates as a basis for their own self-referent praise system.

Summary

The Five Keys to Better Self-Concept are a system for helping children develop the internal mechanism of language for enhancing and maintaining positive self-concept. The Keys are based on the concepts of reinforcement and imitation theory. The role of the teacher is crucial, but it is crucial not in the reinforcements which he provides but in his teaching of pupils to engage in self-referent encouragement and praise.

Chapter **5**

Discipline and Self-Concept Enhancement in the Elementary School

One of the most frequent problems encountered by teachers, parents, and principals in connection with self-concept development is handling discipline problems. In this chapter, techniques for handling discipline problems which minimize damage to the child's self-concept are discussed.

When teachers and other adults use the term *discipline*, they are usually referring to the correction and punishment of a child whose behavior is unacceptable. It is helpful and instructive to look at discipline from the standpoint of the child. A well-disciplined child is not one who is "well punished"; he is one who has characteristics that show that he has learned how to control himself. He is disciplined in the sense of being self-controlled. The major question about discipline is not "Should I spank my children?" but "What can I do so that the child will learn self-control?" Self-control is the major goal of discipline and encompasses a number of other goals which might be called the goals of growing up.

Goals for growing up include the following:

I. Independence
   A. Executive—ability to do things.

   B. Volitional—ability to have own ideas.
   C. Emotional—ability to have ideas and carry them out without
      becoming disturbed.
II. Competence
   A. Intellectual—ability to reason.
   B. Vocational—ability to support oneself.
   C. Social—ability to interact effectively with others.
III. Maturity
   A. In Self-Evaluation—ability to accept oneself.
   B. In Love—ability to love unselfishly.
   C. In Responsibility—ability to accept and evaluate responsi-
      bilities to other people and institutions.
   D. In Values and Goals—ability to set adequate goals and adopt
      adequate values.

   The goals specified for growing up involve increasing control by
the child over his own life. The purpose of any disciplinary action
which adults take should be to get the child to take control of
himself. The purpose of any form of punishment should not be
simple control of the child's behavior. If the aim is to control, it is
sure that the punishment will fail in the long run. It is impossible for
the child to develop maturity and independence within a system in
which control is maintained from the outside. It also is highly
unlikely that this type of outside control will be feasible over the
entire period in which the child is developing adult characteristics.
The process of growing up involves parents and teachers in a
progressive loss of control which becomes increasingly clear during
adolescence. Many adolescent delinquents are referred to authorities
by their parents, because the parents were unable to control them. In
a sense, all parents lose control of their children as the children grow
older. But the basic question is whether or not the child has
developed adequate techniques of self-control, so that when the
parent is not able to control the child the child will have an internal
system that makes outside control unnecessary.
   Another question which disciplinarians continually ask is "Is the
form of correction I'm using being used for my own benefit or for
the child's?" Frequently, punishments, corrections, and attempts at
controlling the child are not undertaken to meet the needs of the
child. Rather, they are aimed toward meeting the needs of the parent
or teacher. There are times when the child's behavior should be
changed to accommodate the needs of an adult. At those times, the
changes should be made when the adult recognizes that they are for
his needs. It is alright to say, "You kids must keep quiet because I

need some peace and quiet." Here the adult is claiming some rights in the adult-child interaction. But to punish the child when the real need or problem (such as a low frustration level) is in the adult is to miss the goals of correction and to fail to cultivate discipline in the child. When punishments are unreasonable in the sense that they are not consistent, the child is in an ambiguous situation. When the punishment does not fit into the pattern of interactions, a clear basis for behavior and punishment is lacking. If the child does not understand the basis for the punishments, he is given an ambiguous learning task. He does not know what it is that he is to learn, and this situation creates a difficult learning situation.

Considering discipline as a factor in learning self-control gives one some basic guidelines for handling failure in the classroom. The failures which the teacher meets are of two types: academic and behavioral. Some children have difficulty learning the appropriate behaviors which are demanded of them in school. And some children have difficulty accomplishing academic tasks. Both situations are failures for the child. One of the primary problems which teachers must face is handling failure situations in such a way that the child learns more self-control and in a way that enhances or maintains a positive self-concept.

Principles of Discipline

The following guidelines are set forth as general principles of discipline which have particular importance for self-concept development. To what principles for handling academic failure can teachers refer?

Arrange a high ratio of successes to failures in academic tasks. The Peanuts cartoon character Charlie Brown is often pictured as the epitome of failure. In a cartoon strip, he was talking about the problem of scraped knees and said something like this: "The sidewalk is the undefeated champ. In over two thousand years of recorded history the sidewalk has never lost a contest with a child's knee!" Many children must look at school the same way. In all their time in school, they have never won. The school and the academic requirements are still the reigning champs. It is the job of the teacher to change this situation so that the child's successes outnumber his failures.

A major task which the teacher faces is how to give success to a child who is performing below normal expectancies. Some of the things which the teacher can do have been discussed in the section on the Keys which deal with goal-setting and evaluation. Even when the teacher is helping the child set realistic goals and self-evaluate in a realistic manner, there are going to be failures. One approach to these failures is to break the task down into small pieces so that there are many smaller goals to achieve. In almost every situation, the child is correct more often than he is wrong. For example, in one training program, teachers were asked to begin marking the correct items on class assignments rather than the wrong items. Also, it was helpful to have the child go back over an assignment when he was having trouble with a few words and actually count the number of words he did know. If the child spells a word incorrectly, the place to start is with the number of letters he had right. It is valuable for a teacher to go through a learning task with a child and to make a note of each correct task that the child does. Even though the final word spelled may not be correct, the child will usually have at least some letters correct; some will have a similar sound to the correct ones; and some will be written neatly. Seldom is the teacher faced with a situation like the one in which a teacher must give a one-word spelling test to a football player with the stipulation that if any letter was right, the player would be admitted to Podunk University. When the player was given the word "coffee," he thought for a moment and spelled, "K-A-U-P-H-Y." Even in such an extreme situation, the teacher could start by saying "Well, you got the first sound right. What other letters do you know that have the same sound as a K?" The point is that in almost any situation there are positive learning possibilities. The ratio of success to failure can be increased if the teacher looks at those positive things and makes them into success instances.

Teach the child ways to avoid the conclusion that failure is typical of him. Failure experiences are often translated into a concept of self. When they are, failure becomes an identifying characteristic of self. The child needs techniques for handling failure so that it does not become a generalized part of the self-concept. This can be done by keeping failure feedback specific to the task failed and by connecting failure with success. Such feedback statements as "You missed four spelling words, but you had six right! Let's aim for seven next week" allow the child to recognize failure without allowing the failure to become overwhelming.

Teach the child self-responsibility for failure. At first, this guideline may seem contradictory to the preceding guideline. Actually, it is not contradictory to say both that the child should avoid generalizing individual failures to a concept that is indicative of him and that the child should take responsibility for individual failures. The latter deals with specifics and the former deals with the conclusions drawn from those specifics. As children learn that they are responsible for their behaviors and actions, they begin to develop a sense of competence. To be in the hands of fate or luck or any force totally outside of one's control is a frightening experience. It is like the feeling of powerlessness that one gets when watching a science fiction movie in which things happen to the helpless characters. It is similar to the feeling one has when one hits a patch of ice in a car—complete helplessness. For long-term self-concept development, the individual needs to develop a sense of control and responsibility. Avoiding failure by blaming it on someone or something else is a nonconstructive way of dealing with the difficult problem of failure. This is not to say that the teacher needs to force the child to admit responsibility. Instead he should teach the child responsibility through active goal-setting and active evaluation of strong and weak points. The child needs help understanding why some days seem to be "bad days," and he needs to rejoice as he sees that he can do something about his performance. Self-responsibility for failure which is developed in a constructive manner need not lead to generalizing failure. Since self-responsibility affects the power to succeed, it can be used as a tool for cultivating a self-concept which includes improvement and success.

Most teachers are more comfortable handling academic failures than they are trying to deal with the behavioral failures of pupils. Teachers generally have greater feelings of competence in academic areas than they have in the area of behavior. Teachers are trained to teach children how to learn and, consequently, they feel comfortable helping children who are having learning difficulties. However, most teachers have received little formal training in dealing with behavioral failure. Frequently, teachers who are working on their master's degree want help learning how to deal with classroom misbehavior or behavioral failure.

Teachers can begin to approach behavioral failure with a degree of confidence if they look at behavioral failure as a failure in learning. Too often teachers approach misbehavior as a motivational or character problem. For example, they think that the child is "trying" to upset the class or that he is "dishonest." These types of judgments rarely help change behavior and are almost never useful when dealing with elementary school age children. The child is learning how to act in life and his failures in behavior should be approached as learning deficits. When the teacher approaches misbehavior as a learning deficit, he is working from his normal strengths. He knows how to teach and can have confidence teaching pupils how to act.

A Strategy for Discipline

The second approach which can give teachers confidence is designating a system they can use to handle situations involving behavioral failures. No system will always work (you will not be able to apply it as you would a cookbook and always have the correct recipe), but a systematic approach does give teachers a place to start. A system provides a starting strategy which will prevent inappropriate discipline, which in turn can cause even more serious problems. Frequently, I hear teachers say, "I wish I had not said that. I don't want to do what I said I was going to do, and I don't know how to get myself out of the situation." If the teacher has a technique available for handling the immediate press of behavioral failures, he can give himself time to make decisions which are more adequate.

The system which I would like to present has been gleaned from a number of places. The primary approach is adapted from lectures by Glasser presented in film (1972). The original work on this approach to discipline and self-concept was done by Prof. Douglas Stanwyck of the University of Maryland, Baltimore County Campus.

The approach is a simple procedure for dealing with classroom behavior that provides children with a way of dealing with their own problem behavior and also that provides for self-concept enhancement.

Follow the outline as each step is discussed.

1. Attend to the child's behavior. The simplest way to attend to the child's behavior and to help him describe his own behavior is to ask the question "What did you do?" A likely answer is "Jamie pushed me" or some other answer which tries to switch the attention from the child's own behavior to someone else's behavior or to some reason for the behavior. The appropriate teacher response is "Yes, but what did you do?" For most children, you will find that after a number of dodges and repetitions of the question they will come up with at least a partial description of what they did. It is important to keep this on the level of behavior. Most adults are not able to deal effectively with motives; they get sidetracked. Although motives could enter the process at some point, it is easier to assess them if there is some description of behavior to fall back on. This situation also assumes that someone saw the child *do* something. If the

Outline of the Plan	Self-Concept Key
1. Have the child describe his behavior.	Key 2: Evaluate realistically
2. Encourage the child to assess his behavior in terms of its helpfulness to others and himself.	Key 2: Evaluate realistically
3. Encourage the child to develop an alternate plan for governing his behavior.	Key 3: Set reasonable goals
4. Have the child sign a statement about his plan.	Key 3: Commitment to goals
5. At the end of the appropriate time period, have the child assess his performance.	Key 2: Evaluate realistically
6. Provide positive reinforcement for those *aspects* of performance that were successful.*	
7. Encourage the child to make a positive statement about his performance.	Key 4: Teach self-praise

*If the child's performance does not meet the criteria set in the plan, return to step 3 and assist the child in modifying his plan so that success is more possible. If, on the other hand, the child's performance was successful, help him develop a more ambitious plan (e.g., for a longer time period or for a larger set of behaviors).

situation is in doubt, the first question is appropriate but it is perhaps not appropriate to keep asking the question. To keep asking the question when you or someone else has not seen the child's behavior frequently puts the child in the position of trying to make up a behavior which he thinks is in line with what you want to hear. Just recently, my teenage daughter told me that when she was in the fourth grade the teacher accused the class of doing something and said they would have to stay after school each day until the child who had done it confessed. The class was convinced that it was someone in another class so they took up a collection and paid one of the boys in the class to confess. To them, it seemed like an equitable solution: The teacher got the confession; the boy was paid for his punishment; and the class was not kept in after school each day. But what did the children learn in the situation? Most likely, it was that "If you give adults what they want to hear, problem situations are solved practically." Remember, if you are in doubt, provide opportunity for describing what was done, but don't push too hard. After the child has described the behavior, you can move to step 2.

2. Encourage the child to assess his behavior in terms of its helpfulness. This is an attempt to help the child evaluate realistically. The criteria of helpfulness is one that should be made explicit. Those behaviors which are assessed as undesirable classroom behaviors are those which are not helpful and, in fact, interfere with accomplishing the goals of the class, whether these goals are set by the teacher or by the pupils. The first and most obvious question is "Did what you did help you?" The answer in a very explosive situation could be "Yes, it made me feel better to kick Jamie!" An appropriate response would be "It made you feel better. But, was it helpful to you?" or "Was it helpful to Jamie?" or "Was it helpful to the class?" or "Was it helpful to me?" Most children would not think kicking a classmate was helpful, even to themselves, because it got them into difficulty with the teacher. At this point, it is appropriate to let the child tell you how he felt it was helpful. He might say something like "I thought it was going to be helpful, but it didn't turn out that way." It would be appropriate to ask him how he thought it might be helpful. Sometimes children do things which are destructive and unacceptable because they are unable to comprehend all of the factors in the situation. One time, my wife and I left our four-year-old daughter with friends over a weekend and, when we came back, they said that she had punched a hole with a nail in a large play ball and was quite upset by the whole episode. After we were home, we asked her why she had done that, and she said that she was playing a game and the ball kept falling into one of the window wells. Since it was hard to get out, she decided to tie a string to it. When she put the nail into the ball to hold the string the ball went flat and wouldn't bounce anymore, and everyone was angry with her. Learning something about how balls are constructed produced the appropriate behavior. The ball was not punctured to destroy it, and this type of behavior must be approached differently than directly destructive behavior. Once the question of helpfulness is handled, you can move on to step 3.

3. Encourage the child to develop an alternative plan for governing his behavior. The plan should have a goal which can be a statement of the appropriate behavior. The plan can be approached with the

question "What do you think you could have done that would have been helpful?" A second part of the plan should be a strategy for reaching that goal. These two steps help the child set realistic goals in relation to his behavior. The plan also should be positive, and it should be attainable and lead to helpful behavior. Some of the plans may not be the best solution, but the teacher should be willing to accept any reasonable solution which the child might make. If he says, "I think I might do better if I did not sit next to Jamie," you should sacrifice the seating chart for the child. The plan should also entail a reasonable time limit. The child could say, "I won't hit Jamie again until lunch." You may want to clarify the meaning, but the time period could be accepted. The plan should contain a statement of what would be acceptable behavior, what would help in reaching that behavior, and a time limit. Once the plan is formulated, it should be written down. Then move to step 4.

4. Have the child sign a statement about his plan. This step deals with the perception of responsibility. One of the primary goals is to cultivate in the child a sense of self-responsibility for behavior, and there is a commitment when he signs his name. Children do not know the legal meaning of contracts and the binding quality of names, but they do know that, when they write their name on something, it means that they are making a promise. Have the child take the paper and keep it to monitor himself. You may say, "Take the paper to your desk and just before lunch you come and tell me how you are doing." Once again, the responsibility is his. He keeps track of his behavior and he reports to you. It may also be helpful to give him a card and say, "Everytime you want to hit someone, put a check mark on this card and then at lunch time we can see how many times you kept yourself from hitting people."

5. At the end of the time period in the contract, have the child assess his performance. How did he do? What problems did he have? Were there times when he thought he was not going to be able to do what he wanted to do? How did he handle those times? Once again, this process helps the child to evaluate realistically.

6. Provide positive reinforcement for those aspects of the child's performance which were successful. If his performance has not been totally successful, look for elements of his activity that indicate progress. If you are looking at this as a learning problem, look for the positive points upon which you can build a learning sequence.

7. Encourage the child to make positive statements about his performance. This is a direct application of Key Four: Teach Children to Praise Themselves.

Things to Avoid

Two things which are likely to occur frequently should be avoided. Excuses are one thing to be avoided. The key to self-control is self-responsibility, and many adults and children who do not exercise adequate control over their behavior adopt the mechanism of denying that they are responsible for their behavior. Therefore in all of the steps, there needs to be an emphasis on self-responsibility and self-control. The second thing to avoid is punishment. There may be some situations in which punishment seems appropriate, but it tends to interfere with positive learning. When children become accustomed to punishment and expect it, it loses its effectiveness. My wife and I have taken care of foster children for a number of years and have consistently found that the more punishment the child has had the less effective punishment is as a deterrent to unacceptable behavior. Children whom you would be tempted to punish most because their behavior is most persistently unacceptable are the children who will be least deterred by punishment. And those children with whom punishment would be effective can be helped by other means. Generally, methods other than physical punishment and harsh scolding can be effective in correcting unacceptable behavior.

These are suggestions for developing a system or technique for handling behavior failures. However, a few cautions should be given before you try it in the classroom. When teachers talk about handling behavior failures, they almost always have a particular child in mind. This child is usually the terror of the school. No teacher has been able to handle him, and each teacher lives in dread of the day when he becomes a part of the class. As you look at this system for handling behavior problems, you have either thought, "It won't work with So-and-So!" or, "I'll try it on So-and-So and see if it really works."

Do not try a new technique on the class terror. You will be in the process of learning a new approach, and when you are learning something new you should maximize the possibility of your success, just as you want to maximize the success possibilities for your pupils. Start with a relatively easy behavior problem and try out the technique a few times to give yourself an opportunity to see some of the difficulties. Get some practice in the types of responses that children are likely to make. Give yourself an opportunity to feel competent and comfortable using the technique. You may find that the child with severe behavior failure will begin to ask you why you are not having him write out what he wants to do. You can respond, "Well, Chuck, you are not ready for that yet." When you feel comfortable and see that the system and technique works, you can make adjustments to fit your own teaching style. Then begin to tackle some of the more difficult behavior problems using the same technique.

Summary

One of the most difficult problems for the teacher is handling failure in an appropriate way. The failure exhibited by elementary pupils is of two types: academic and behavioral. Both of these types of failure are problems of inadequate or inappropriate learning. The teacher is faced with the task of maintaining a suitable classroom environment while he teaches the children the appropriate behavior. A technique is presented which attempts to handle failure problems in a manner which will be self-enhancing to the child who has the failure problems.

Chapter 6

Self-Concept Development
during Adolescence

The process of development during the elementary school years is one of moving from instability toward increasing stability. As the child goes from kindergarten to the late elementary grades, he becomes more stable in his behavior and is more predictable. He has learned the types of behavior that lead to consistency and control. His academic work is more predictable because he has acquired more skills and knowledge. He has had more social experiences and has learned the societal skills necessary for getting along with other children and the greatly enlarged number of adults whom he encounters in school. His physical development has advanced, and he has more control over his body. Boys and girls have developed a measure of coordination so that they can do tasks without awkwardness. They play basketball and other games with increasing control and accuracy.

Adolescence dramatically changes this pleasant picture. For the teacher who sees children enter adolescence, it sometimes seems as though all their effort was for nothing. One teacher said, "This fifth grade class was the best class I ever had and I thought that sixth grade was just going to be super. But then over the summer about five or six of the leaders hit early adolescence!" The sixth grade class tended to be moody, loud, and scatterbrained.

During adolescence, there is an increased drive for change in the individual. The increased change and corresponding lack of stability brings with it a need for reorganization of the self-concept. This chapter will concentrate on the unique factors which enter development at adolescence and require a reorganization of the self-concept. The unique factors which comprise adolescence produce a *new view of self.* There will also be an emphasis on what teachers can do to help the adolescent maintain a positive self-concept in the face of change and to develop methods of enhancing the self.

In research with children and adolescents, the author has found that there are six parts or factors in self-concept (Stanwyck & Felker, 1971; Stanwyck, 1972). These six factors are behavior, anxiety, intellectual or school status, appearance, happiness, and satisfaction. Each of these six factors is dramatically affected by pubescence and entering adolescence.

In this discussion of adolescence, it will be assumed that adolescence is a psycho-social-biological phenomenon. That is, adolescence is the name that is given to all the psychological and social changes that take place when the child enters puberty. Some of these changes are the direct result of the physiological changes of puberty, such as change in appearance due to increased height and size. Other changes are the result of the way in which society views physiological changes, for example, the push by society for the individual to be independent when he reaches reproductive maturity. Other changes are psychological in the sense that the individual behaves differently than he did as a child. Some of the adolescent's behaviors are based on increased physiological drive combined with different social perception. It is well to remember that adolescence is a combination of factors. The concept that all behavior is purposive and that the causes of behavior are multiple, interrelated, and complex applies to the phenomena of adolescence. One cannot point to one single cause for the dramatic changes that take place following puberty. Most behavior changes are precipitated by physiological changes, but reactions to these physiological changes differ dramatically from society to society.

It has been argued that the reactions to adolescence in western culture are among the most severe because of the discontinuous training which western cultures foster. That is, there are a number of behaviors which are stressed in training children that are opposite to what is expected of individuals as adults. For example, dependency training for children when individuals are expected to be independent as adults points to one area of discontinuous training. Adolescence involves a dramatically different set of factors and relationships than those present in childhood. The adolescent is different and there are different expectations. There are also changes in behavior.

Adolescent Behavior

The adolescent is characterized by increased instability because of the behavioral changes that accompany puberty. For example, adolescents are usually more moody. In boys particularly, there is an increase in aggressive outbursts. Adolescent instability is characterized by more frequent verbal outbursts and by interactions which indicate increased frustration and lowered frustration tolerance. It has been argued (McCandless, 1967) that the increase in dramatic outbursts is due partly to an increase in the level of frustrating stimuli. That is, there are more areas in which there is a blocking of goal-oriented behavior. The adolescent wants to do more things which he is not allowed to do. The increased frustration is also due partly to sexual drive and the prohibitions against sexual expression, but the outbursts also are increased partly by the fact that the tolerance for frustration is lowered, and the individual is more sensitive to outside stimuli. It is like having a sore toe—it can hurt because more people hit it, and it can hurt simply because the same bumps which were ignored in the past now hurt. The adolescent faces both factors: he is more sensitive, and people are more frustrating.

The result of increased frustration is that adolescents are likely to be more moody and mouthy. He is likely to be more apt to blow up and have unexplainable aggressive outbursts. She is likely to have more fits of crying and screaming.

Adolescent behavioral changes are also likely to be sex-oriented, because the primary characteristics of puberty are psycho-sexual. At puberty, the individual is able to bear or father children, and the corresponding drives which increase the likelihood of reproduction enter human experience. There is greater sexual awareness and attraction. The adolescent is likely to be more aware of sex stimuli, and sex stimuli which were always present are going to be more arousing than they were before puberty. The sex drive is an extremely strong and pervasive motivating force in the life of the adolescent. To ignore its influence on self-concept is to ignore a vital factor.

Adolescent behavior is increasingly characterized by independence and behaviors which show that independence is being sought. Ausubel (1954) compared the interactions of adolescent and parent with the interactions between a parent and a two-year-old. The two-year-old is one who is fighting for freedom. He is moving from the period when he was king of the realm and when his wish was practically law in the family to a period when the pressures of conforming are imposed. He fights this pressure, but the most likely outcome is that he will conform and that he will give up his independent status for a position of security. The two-year-old is noted for his heightened negativism and his temper tantrums. The period contains heightened pressures for both parent and child. The adolescent period is noted for the same characteristics. There are more verbal outbursts (temper tantrums), increased pressure from both parent and child as they strive for greater control (generation gap), and increased unwillingness for the adolescent to do what he is told (negativism). Although there are notable similarities between the two struggles for independence, the outcomes are dramatically different. The two-year-old almost always loses, and the adolescent almost always wins.

It has been suggested that the greatest value of textbooks on adolescence is that they give the parents something to do while the adolescent becomes an adult! There may be some value in that function, because the only outcome which is ultimately acceptable is that the adolescent win his struggle for independence. Most parents want their children to become independent, but they also feel that somehow they can let the adolescent make independent decisions on the one hand and ensure on the other hand that he will make the right decisions. There simply is no way that can be. The adolescent must become independent if he is not going to be a developmental failure. Too often the struggle for independence is characterized by a disregard for other persons in the situation and this can lead to a struggle that is intense and bitter. One way to avoid such a bitter struggle is to offer training for independence in childhood.

The changes in adolescent behavior require a reorganization of self-concept. The child developed stable ways of perceiving himself and, if his behavior dramatically changes, these learned perceptions are out of harmony with what he sees in himself, and a reorganization of his self-perceptions is required.

Anxiety in Adolescence

The psycho-physiological changes which characterize adolescence also bring on anxiety. There are two major causes for anxiety in adolescence. One is the internal problem of dealing with the changes that have taken place. The drives of sexuality bring new feelings, new emotions, and new desires, and it is a difficult task to accept them and to understand them. The task is magnified for many adolescents by the feeling that the drives and emotions are in charge of them and that they are at the mercy of some uncontrollable inner force. It has been pointed out that what the adolescent in puberty fears is a loss of control over his drives (Holmes, 1964). Adults in the adolescent's environment also present him with the same fear. He fears that, if he allows adults to help him, he may lose control and give his independence, which has been gained with some effort, back to the adults from whom he has gained it. What he is struggling against is a fear of loss of control, and many times he reacts with hostility and high general anxiety to this fear. Hostility is often born of insecurity and fear. Holmes (1964) has noted from his long association and work with disturbed adolescents that all adolescents have symptoms of disturbance and that most of them handle the pressures well enough to avoid classification as being "disturbed." Holmes also notes that with gentle reassurance almost any thirteen-year-old will acknowledge that he frequently suffers grave doubts about his sanity (Holmes, 1964). The adolescent must fight to overcome chronic confusion and, although he is distrustful of giving himself back into the hands of adults, he is even more distrustful of himself.

The second major cause of anxiety is the ambiguous situation in which the adolescent finds himself. Adolescents are neither fish nor fowl. They are neither children nor adults. They live on the fence of being told to grow up on one side and being denied the activities which they see grown-ups around them doing on the other. If you want to perceive what is meant by this living on a fence, try to explain to an adolescent when he will be an adult. You find that saying "the age of twenty-one" does not work since that age is only a chronological age and they are expected to act like adults long before twenty-one. You will soon find that trying to define adulthood by emotional maturity forces you to classify some friends and relatives who occupy adult roles as nonadults since they are relatively immature. If you try to describe it physically, your description breaks down when you look up and find that a sixteen- or seventeen-year-old (thanks to excellent baby care) is two inches taller and 20 pounds heavier than you and is actually in much better physical condition than you. Obviously, it is difficult to answer the question "When will I be an adult?" But this is the situation in which the adolescent finds himself: Day after day he is supposed to strive to become an adult, and yet no one can tell him how he will know when he has reached his goal. The absence of specific and visible end points forces the adolescent into an ambiguous situation, and it explains why some symbols of adulthood become so important. The driver's license takes on significance far greater than is implied by the few times when the adolescent is actually given the car to use. Graduation from high school has a symbolism beyond the mere completion of a course of study. Although other societies have formal rites which clearly tell the adolescent that he is an adult, American society is characterized by informal rites which adolescents themselves construct. This situation tends to leave the adolescent in an extremely ambiguous situation, and ambiguity fosters anxiety. If an individual doesn't know where he is going or if he doesn't know that he is ever going to make it, he is likely to become anxious.

Intellectual Abilities and School Status

There are also changes in intellectual abilities and school status. During the early and middle elementary school years, those children who are the dependable, consistent doers of what the teacher wants are those who receive the most reinforcements from both the teacher and the peer group. The teacher is such a powerful force that the determinations of peer standing are in most cases strongly influenced by the standing which the child has in the eyes of the teacher. When the child reaches late elementary school and early high school, the situation changes, and the peer group begins making its own judgments. Peer group judgments are made on slightly different criteria than those of the teacher. Although the teacher still prefers the conformer, the peers give some status to the rebel. The increased emphasis which the adolescent places on his own independence leads him to look for independence in those to whom he is going to give status.

The adolescent also increases his intellectual activity, and he is more able to consider ideas abstractly and on a theoretical level. In addition, he is able to handle intellectual matter without high personal involvement so that he can consider an idea which may be diametrically opposed to a personally held value (Ausubel, 1954). In addition, he can test other values and ideas without giving himself to them. The adolescent also is able to use more abstract language with which to investigate himself. He can look at himself in more abstract terms and describe himself with a more complex set of variables. Although complexity of self-concept has not been investigated by researchers, it has been suggested as a central feature of self-concept (McCandless, 1967). As the ability to look at more facets increases, the individual must work to reorganize his self-concept to take into account a wider range of variables. These changes interact with parental reaction and social status to give the adolescent another area of rapid change and disruption with which he has to deal.

Physical Appearance and Adolescence

There are changes in physical appearance. During the adolescent growth spurt which precedes and accompanies other aspects of puberty, there is a rather dramatic increase in growth rate. Although this increase is not dramatic compared to the growth of the newborn, it is dramatic compared to the rate of growth in the late childhood period. There is a rapid increase in height and, for many children, this increase in height is accompanied by distinguishable changes in facial features as the face becomes elongated and loses its round baby shape. Boys begin to grow facial hair, and girls show recognizable breast development. All of these are changes to which the individual must adapt. All age groups show changes in appearance as they grow, but the changes normally take place slowly enough to allow comfortable adjustment, and individuals tend not to notice the changes. But for the adolescent who is facing the rapid changes of puberty, the physical changes are very noticeable, and he becomes different enough that he must reorganize the way in which he looks at himself. Although growing up is a good thing, the actual process is difficult. The adolescent boy may find that as his appearance changes he loses some of his appeal. The adolescent girl may find that as she enters womanhood the round pudgy face which everyone thought was so cute is no longer looked upon as desirable. Both boys and girls may find that facial blemishes are a constant problem and that their faces look different in a negative way. In all of these and in many other small ways, the adolescent is faced with a remaking of his self-image.

Happiness Isn't Adolescence

The rapid and difficult changes sometimes make it almost impossible for adolescents to be happy. Although adults tend to idealize adolescence in poetry and fiction, people who are asked whether they would like to relive their adolescence overwhelmingly answer "no" (Jersild, 1963). They would not want to go through adolescence again even if they could do it knowing everything they know now. Adolescents feel emotions deeply and intensely and have spurts of intense joy, but they also feel sorrow and heartbreak just as intensely. Someone has said that the beginning of puppy love is the start of a dog's life. The problems of heterosexual adjustment and the uneasiness of being overlooked is not a happy time. In all of these areas, the child who is happy when he enters adolescence and enters adolescence with a positive self-concept has the best chance of weathering the assaults.

Satisfaction

Another major change is in the area of satisfaction. Much of what is called satisfaction is dependent upon the ability to perform tasks which are perceived as appropriate and to which an individual decided to give his energies. My daughter was taking advanced accelerated algebra and had a perfect paper on the final. After I talked with her about it and complimented her, she said, "I'm really happy about it and pleased because I worked so hard for it." Part of her satisfaction was in the fact that she had given herself to the task. If she had received a prize that was straight luck, she would have been pleased but she would not have felt "satisfaction." One of the difficulties which adolescents find in the area of satisfaction is that, as the requirements around them become ambiguous, they are not able to work toward the requirements with a high degree of involvement. One cannot work diligently for a goal that is not specified. It is difficult to feel satisfied if the feedback as to whether one is making progress is vague and ambiguous.

The Effects of Adolescence

The adolescent is faced with ambiguity which influences all of the areas of his performance and development. This ambiguity has a dramatic effect on self-concept development. It was found in a longitudinal/cross-sectional study that girls had a dramatic drop in self-concept level between the seventh and eighth grades (Stanwyck, 1972). The most likely explanation for this is that the effects of adolescence were taking their toll. It also has been found that there is a high degree of stability when you look at self-concept in preadolescence and in late adolescence (Carlson, 1965). The most likely explanation is that self-concept takes a drop as puberty has its effect and then the self-concept tends to recover. Those who have positive self-concepts recover the most. In dealing with the changes at puberty and the maintenance of a positive self-concept, the adolescent is faced with maintaining or building a sense of belonging, a sense of competence, and a sense of worth. *Building* the self-concept is specifically mentioned. Although dramatic changes produce problems of adjustment, changes also clear the stage and give an opportunity for relearning. But the resulting relearning can be destructive when the adolescent changes his self-concept in a negative way. However, the opportunity for relearning also allows changes in a positive direction. When the adolescent is forced to reorganize his self-concept, he is given a chance to reorganize it in a more positive direction. This new chance is particularly necessary if efforts to change the self-concept have been unsuccessful during childhood. Adolescence may be the last chance for dealing with the individual in a fluid, changing situation.

The Sense of Belonging. The road to independence is frightening. Although independence has its attractions, it has its fearful elements. It is like areas of pre-columbian maps that were marked "This place is inhabited by dragons and monsters." Independence means responsibility and facing the consequences of one's actions. In order to be independent, the individual adolescent must break with his parents. Some writers refer to this break as "emancipation" (Ausubel, 1954). Although emancipation may be too strong a word because it suggests that the parents own and completely dominate the child during childhood, it does point up the important fact that an individual cannot be dependent upon the wishes of his parents and be independent at the same time. The adolescent need not break with the desires of the parents and engage in actions which are contrary to their wishes, but he must achieve volitional independence so that he will be able to make up his own mind. Because of parental training, modeling, and identification, his ideas may be very similar to those of his parents, but the important factor which shows adolescent independence is that the conclusions are reached on some basis other than parental desires. The adolescent who uses parental desires as one factor to be considered and then evaluates all of the factors involved is displaying a high degree of independence and maturity.

The volitional and behavioral break with the parents brings with it the sharp question "To whom and with whom do I belong?" The child frequently develops the security of feeling that he is Mother's boy or Daddy's boy. But when he is no longer tied to his parents, who is he? One of the most frequent struggles within adolescents is with the question "Who am I?" It is not a question that can be answered with name, rank, and serial number. Identification with a larger unit, such as an army, fraternity, or sorority club, etc., helps many young men and women develop an identity separate from the identity which they have as members of a family. When the adolescent willfully breaks away from the parents, he is faced with the same problems which he had at age two when he was struggling with his parents. He must find answers to the questions "Where do I find security?" and "Where do I find acceptance?" Much of the devotion of adolescents to groups and individuals outside the adult family structure is an attempt to find suitable answers to these two questions. Most adolescents have competing surrogates for the security and acceptance of the family.

The most obvious surrogate for the family is the peer group. By giving himself to the peer group and investing in the peer group such factors as status, reinforcement power, coercion ability, and source of values, the adolescent is claiming for himself these factors rather than allowing them to continue to reside in his parents. He is also saying that he has something else to which he belongs since he perceives that belonging exclusively to the family is too confining to his development.

The adolescent frequently uses other individuals as a source of belonging in addition to the peer group. Intense heterosexual relationships in adolescence frequently take the direction of "It is you and me against the world. No matter what happens we always have each other. We belong to each other." Independence seems to be more a struggle for the boy, because there is more pressure on him to be independent. Thus his girlfriend's family often serves as a place for belonging. He spends time in the girl's home; he is taken on picnics and family outings; and he takes part in the holiday celebrations of the girl's family. Occasionally, he picks a girl from an all-girl family so that he does in fact fill a vacant spot in the girl's family and feels as though he belongs.

Occasionally, the adolescent gives himself to causes to gain a kind of belonging. Hoffer (1951) pointed out that giving one's self unreservedly to causes is a means of self-enhancement. It should be noted that all of these mechanisms are for finding security and acceptance in a period when, at least from the viewpoint of the adolescent, he is losing the security derived from the sense of belonging to the parents.

The Sense of Competence. The adolescent has greatly increased abilities. He is stronger and more physically mature and, once he adjusts to his increased size and physical growth, he has increased coordination. From the viewpoint of society, he has increased ability to work and produce something which is worth wages. In spite of his increased ability and competence, the adolescent's sense of competence comes under increasing attack during adolescence.

Adolescents tend to overestimate their ability. This is exemplified by the inflated sense of coordination which adolescents perceive they have in driving skills. Their coordination is better than it will ever be, but they are not as quick as they think they are. They also overestimate the status which they are going to occupy. They want to be considered on a par with adults as far as status is concerned, but they do not receive this status from the adult community. They are still kids in the eyes of society.

The ambiguity is not all in the eyes of the adults. Most adolescents want to fluctuate between adult status and the security of an all-teenage peer community. The corresponding overestimation of ability by the adolescent and the underestimation of ability by the community produces an assault on the adolescent's self-concept which is particularly evident in his sense of competence.

America's highly specialized society has increasingly placed emphasis on high level skills; a fact which has magnified the problem of maintaining an adolescent's sense of competence. Society has emphasized that more education is necessary and that jobs without high school diplomas are hard to come by. In fact, society has emphasized more and more education to the point that many adolescents feel that they are incompetent and, for that matter, that anyone is incompetent if they do not have more education. The emphasis on education as a prerequisite for production has also made opportunities for adolescent employment sparse. The range of competence or the areas in which the adolescent can show that he is competent have decreased. In most cases, the area in which competence can be shown is almost totally limited to the school situation and the attendant extracurricular activities. The adolescent who does not perform well in school and is not involved in extracurricular activities has few places where he can show that he is competent.

The Sense of Worth. When the child first moves into the school situation, the basis for the sense of worth centers more on competence than on belonging. The child shows that he is competent in dealing with objects, peers, and adults, and he strengthens his sense of worth. During adolescence, the individual is faced with the problem of how to develop and maintain the sense of worth when the sense of belonging and sense of competence are both under stress. The drive for independence causes doubt about the adolescent's sense of belonging. Attacks on his perceived competence by society and particularly by significant others in society call into question his sense of competence.

The adolescent may perceive that adults think less of him than the adults actually do. But once again, the important influence on self-concept is what the adolescent perceives, not on what is actually occurring in the environment. The adolescent's perception of a low opinion by adults threatens his own senses of belonging, competence, and worth. The child could give himself a sense of self-worth and self-status on the basis of the status which he had in the eyes of his parents, but this is no longer possible for the adolescent. Society in many open and subtle ways indicates that the adolescent must stand on his own two feet, which means that he is standing on his own status, which is low.

Holmes (1964) has described the bludgeoning which the self-concept takes during adolescence:

> In this highly experimental and uncommitted phase of his life, the adolescent has little which is permanent and reliable upon which to construct a stable conception of what he is like and how much he is worth. He has no job or career by which he can be named; no house, spouse, or children; no definitive office in the church; or respectable place in the politics and community affairs of the adults. Many of his tasks bear the stamp of "made work," exercises to strengthen him for future labors. He longs with mixed feelings for a real job, at one moment firmly convinced of his competence and at the next gravely doubting that he could last for twenty-four hours on his own without starving to death.

In addition to the attacks on self-concept brought about by a feeling of incompetence, there are also the attacks which come about by failures in decision making. The adolescent is faced with the complex task of making his own moral decisions. In addition to inadequate training and practice in how to make moral judgments, the adolescent is caught up in the process of showing others and himself that he, and not his parents, is now making the moral judgments. The only way that he can be sure that he is making his own decisions, and consequently that others such as peers can be sure, is to make decisions which are at odds with his parents' values.

These pressures make many of the moral judgments of adolescents inadequate. The inadequacy is seen not only by external judges in the community but also by adolescents themselves. It is interesting also that many of the values of adolescents are very similar to the values which his parents have. This is probably due to the fact that American culture fosters identification with parents and that part of the identification process in infancy is an adoption of the set of values espoused by the parents. In most cases in which the adolescent is struggling against a set of values which his parents have, he also is fighting against the set of values which he has internalized. In a real sense, he is struggling with himself. If he makes decisions which are out of harmony with those values, he is apt to feel guilty and unworthy.

Many of the feelings of unworthiness which the individual has in adolescence are influenced by decisions involving sexuality. Sexual fantasies and sexual behavior, both homosexual and heterosexual, are common in early adolescence. Masturbation is an almost constant concern for adolescent boys. Attempts to make decisions in the context of strong drives, internalized values, and a struggle for independence are bound to lead to decisions which are looked upon by the adolescent himself as immoral.

Helping Adolescents

What can teachers do to help students through adolescence? The first thing that teachers can do is to try to accurately describe the behavior of the adolescent and then try to see the situation from the viewpoint of the adolescent. Attempts by teachers to see situations from other viewpoints are applicable in all stages of development, but this approach is particularly important when working with adolescents because adolescents are more likely to see things in a distorted manner. The general conflicts with which the adolescent must deal tend to give him tunnel vision. He sees everything from a narrow perspective and the teacher outside of that perspective sees a different world. It is impossible for the teacher to see the world precisely as the adolescent sees it, but the teacher can come a lot closer if he takes the time to try.

You may find it helpful at this point to go back to the diagram on page 27. Remember that you are on the outside and the adolescent is feeling, hurting, and perceiving. Try to get at least a glimpse of what he is perceiving. This general approach is necessary since any techniques which could be suggested are dependent upon your accurately assessing the situation. If you are unable to perceive the situation in a way close to how the adolescent is perceiving it, you are dealing with one situation and he is responding to another.

Some Suggestions on How Teachers Can Help. Grant him some independence of choice while including expressions of affection, belonging, and worth. Remember that one of his most difficult tasks is to become independent and yet feel as though he belongs. In all stages of development, the teacher and parent need to break away from regarding the worth of children in an extrinsic manner. Too often, the worth of the individual child is determined by what he can do or what he will do. "You are a worthwhile person" is too often connected with "because you do good things." In adolescence, the individual knows that things that he does are not good even by his own standards, and frequently draws the conclusion that he is not a worthwhile person.

One distinct advantage which the adolescent has is that he can use language and he may frustrate you by using this language to defend himself. The typical "I don't know!" responses can turn you off. But the adolescent is far ahead of the two-year-old who has learned only screaming to get what he wants. The language base of the adolescent is greatly expanded, and he uses this language in a more introspective manner than the young child. Adults who are working with adolescents can help them use their own language as a tool for seeing themselves. Describing and explaining is one way of seeing.

The greater use of language also means that the adolescent can begin to see that actions are behavioral expressions of feelings. Frequently, an adolescent will say, "I could not see that what you were doing was best for me and I thought you were only trying to put me down, but now I can see that it was something for my good and you were doing it because you loved me." It may take some hard knocks before he begins to see that this is true. The ability to see the relationship between an emotion, such as love, and the corresponding behavior that goes with it is something that takes a high level of reasoning. Language with which to do the reasoning is a crucial advantage.

Explain to adolescents what is happening in their stage of development. In general, teachers do a poor job of informing children about the physical-sexual-emotional changes that will happen to them at adolescence. The ambiguity of adolescence can be reduced by accurate information and understanding. The adolescent girl needs to know that the period between 11-13 is the only time in human development in which the girls are bigger and heavier than the boys. She needs to know that the adolescent growth spurt of an early maturing girl makes her larger than the boys but that the boys will catch up. It is unlikely that she will always be the tallest, strongest person in her class. The late maturing boy needs to know that he will have a growth spurt and that he will tend to catch up with the group eventually.

Such information is valuable for all adolescents in helping them cope with the changes in themselves—they need to see themselves as normal if they are going to maintain a positive self-concept. Although you may feel that you are not making much progress, it is heartwarming to find that your students use the same information to quiet the fears of classmates who do not have the same knowledge that you have given them.

The information which can be helpful to adolescents is not restricted to the area of physiology. They can be helped by information on how adults feel and how adults handle their emotions. If adolescents are going to imitate adult behaviors, they need information from adults that they can use to imitate the mature reactions which adults have developed. Techniques that you have learned for dealing with your emotions and frustrations can be helpful to the adolescent. Helping him find something that is in keeping with the individual's personality is important. One adolescent may like to withdraw; another may like to talk things out; and another may find that keeping busy is useful. But the adult can help by introducing the child and adolescent to these approaches and by explaining why they work and helping the adolescent try them in times of stress.

The adolescent needs to be told that the emotions, frustrations, and passions of adolescence are normal, that they can be controlled, and that help is available from adults. This information and concern will help the adolescent view himself as normal and will help him see that there are ways that he can prevent loss of control over the things that are happening to him.

The adolescent needs controlled opportunities to prove his competencies. Normally, it would be much easier for families if the adolescent did not take the responsibility of a job. For many families, the adolescent's job is more trouble than it is worth in the sense of financial feedback into the family. Sometimes, the car must be shared, or special arrangements must be made for vacations. The amounts earned, if totally saved, could provide relief at some later date, but they are usually spent on immediate needs and pleasures. In spite of the inconvenience, the need for opportunities to demonstrate competence is great. The adolescent must observe that he or she can do things. They need the thrill of getting the paycheck and deciding how it can be spent. And they need the satisfaction of saving for something they would not get if they did not work for it. At the same time, it should be clear that this is a learning process. The early adolescent is apt to try to do too much and to have high expectations. One adolescent with whom I worked closely always had the maximum possible amount of money that could be earned figured out and planned on. Since people usually make a salary closer to the mean than the maximum, he was continually disappointed in his performance and received little satisfaction from his rewards. The problem of setting unrealistic goals and expectations continued to plague him throughout adolescence.

Help adolescents by letting them see that much adult decision making is not a choice between one absolute good and one absolute bad. One of the aspects which plagues the adolescent's feeling of worth is the constant dissatisfaction with his own judgments. While dissatisfaction is appropriate, feelings of unworthiness and the generalization of this dissatisfaction to the self-concept are not desirable. One of the difficulties with making moral judgments is that individuals frequently are placed in the position of making choices between two conflicting right things or a choice between two things which are less than ideal. Frequently, adolescents are dissatisfied with their judgments because they evaluate their choices as though they were choosing between perfect and anything less. One way in which the adolescent can be helped is to be shown that many adult decisions are based on perceptions of the situation as it really is and not on some imaginary ideal situation. This does not mean that judgments are to be made without standards, but it does mean that the standards must have something to do with the real activities of life.

In all of the suggestions which have been made, there is a continuing emphasis on using language to maintain a positive self-concept. This language is used to make judgments. Language is used to set goals and to give feedback to the individual and to explain to the individual his situation. It also has been found helpful to give adolescents an opportunity to understand themselves by attempting to understand someone else and attempting to help someone else. One teacher has taught a course on self-concept enhancement for adolescents using the Five Keys to Better Self-Concept as an outline of the course. Each adolescent had to find a younger child he could help for five weeks by tutoring him. They were to try to help the child learn to evaluate realistically and to set reasonable goals. They were also to teach the child to praise himself and to praise others. At the end of the course, they were to write a final report based on a diary of what happened and what they thought as things developed over the five weeks.

The final reports revealed a number of interesting things. One was that the younger children had sharply increased performance. A couple of the elementary teachers asked that the program be continued because it was doing so much good for the elementary pupils. A second outcome was that many of the adolescents began to apply the Five Keys to their own lives and found that it provided positive self-enhancement. They specifically and frequently pointed out that they had begun to look at what they were doing to themselves as they tried to help a younger child develop better ways of treating himself or herself.

One of the primary conclusions drawn from this teaching experience was that adolescents can be taught and need to be taught ways of defending themselves against the changes that produce attacks on the self-concept. It also was concluded that the Five Keys is one way of helping them to develop positive ways of dealing with themselves and that helping another person is an effective approach.

Summary

Adolescence produces a number of changes which require modification or reorganization of the self-concept. The changes present an opportunity for positive reorganization, but they also bring difficulties. The adolescent can be helped by learning new ways of maintaining a sense of competence, belonging, and worth. The positive understanding of what is happening to him during this period is a means of developing positive views of self as is the process of helping a younger child develop the Five Keys.

Conclusions

T he central assumption of this book has been that it is good for children to have a positive view of themselves. This positive view of self forms the platform upon which other positive learning experiences can be built.

The child who thinks about himself in a negative way and learns to attach negative terms to himself is quite likely to have a difficult time viewing any experience as being good or positive. Recently, I was watching a group of children playing in the yard. They had a number of pieces of colored plastic from a table game and had found a new use for them. They had discovered that if you look through a piece of colored plastic the color of everything you look at is changed. They were having a great time looking at things and seeing odd colors as their vision was filtered through the colored plastic. Similarly, the self-concept is also a filtering and coloring mechanism in human experience. If it is negative, everything which is seen in the world takes on a negative hue. If it is positive, it provides the basis for seeing things in the world in a positive way. This aspect of self-concept makes the development of a positive self-concept one of the crucial developmental goals for children.

The development of the self-concept is going on when other learning experiences seem to be in the foreground. As the child learns language, he is learning a set of words which provide the pool from which he can choose words to apply to himself. If he learns only negative words, he will use them on himself and others. My four-year-old son picked up the word "dummy" and was going around applying it to himself when he did something at which he was not successful. We have helped him to find a different word and to regard dummy as a bad word that should not be used. As the child learns to handle his physical skills and equipment, he is learning to regard himself as competent or incompetent. As he learns to handle his emotion, he is learning to view himself as one who has control or as one who is powerless.

The all-pervasive nature of the learning and development of a self-concept makes helping children to see themselves in a positive manner one of the primary tasks of the teacher. Everyone wants children to grow up to be competent and to enjoy learning to use these competencies in life. The learning of a positive self-concept is one of the central tasks involved in such a learning experience.

In spite of the central importance of the self-concept, it frequently is something that is overlooked in handling of other experiences. Simply because the learning of the self-concept goes on all the time, adults fail to give attention to it and do not go about structuring experiences so that a positive self-concept is learned by the young. Few persons purposefully try to make a child feel incompetent, unworthy, or unloved, but these attitudes and learnings are frequently communicated. This occurs when adults let themselves become so engrossed with teaching the child something that they forget to give attention to what is being taught about the self. At times, they become so intent upon teaching the child not to make the same mistake again that they put too much emphasis on the mistake and unknowingly teach the child that he is a person who "always makes mistakes." Adults become so concerned about the child learning some aspect of proper behavior that they unwittingly communicate to the child that they think he is "a bad person." They become involved in trying to teach the child something or so intent upon what they are doing that they give the child the impression that he is an outsider who is "butting in where he doesn't belong." When teachers and other adults engage in such behaviors with children, they are acting in a way which is self-defeating. Yet, they do it not out of purpose but because they fail to look for the self-concept learning that is going on in these interactions.

It is well to frequently ask ourselves what our children and pupils are learning about their competence, their belonging, and their worth. When one asks this, it brings one back to looking at this important aspect of learning. Every individual who has the opportunity to work with children has a relatively brief time in which he can be an influence on the child. But the influence on the self-concept will endure for many years. The self-concept once it is formed becomes a major determinant in how the individual sees things in the world. The period of infancy and childhood and the influential people will be of great importance to the child's self-concept development.

The major portion of this book has dealt with a method for helping children develop more positive self-concepts. The method is based on the cultivation of self-reinforcing and self-encouraging language in the life of the child. This cultivation is carried on through Five Keys or principles of positive self-concept development.

1. Adults, praise yourselves.
2. Help children to evaluate realistically.
3. Teach children to set reasonable goals.
4. Teach children to praise themselves.
5. Teach children to praise others.

This approach to self-concept enhancement is a learning approach and is based on the idea that children learn by imitation in addition to direct teaching. It also has safeguards against the development of self-centeredness or egotism by emphasizing reasonable evaluation and goal-setting. My five-year-old son came into the house recently and showed my wife a piece of scribbled paper. He said, "Isn't that good writing, Mom?" Mom replied, "No, that is not writing. But it is good scribbling and that is how a five-year-old learns to write. He first learns how to be a good scribbler." Jeff walked away and then said to his sister, "Look, Linda, isn't this good scribbling? I think it is!" The aim of self-concept enhancement is not to have children unrealistically ignore those things that need development and improvement but to realistically look at themselves and their competence and worth.

The principles and ideas which have been presented are action ideas. They are not meant to be talked about, although it makes interesting discussion to drop some of the ideas into adult conversation. Basically, the Keys are ideas which only you, the teacher, can translate into actions which will help the children with whom you come into contact. To put the ideas into an action plan will take concentrated effort on your part. Adults do not naturally do those things which will help children be more positive toward themselves. You live in an evaluation- and competition-centered environment which works against many of the things which have been discussed in this book. But it is encouraging that you as one individual can have a dramatic and lasting effect on the lives of individual children with whom you work. It is this long-lasting influence which the author hopes will be the result of your putting into practice in your classroom the Five Keys to Better Self-Concept.

Bibliography

Allee, J. G. (Ed.) *Webster's dictionary of the American language.* Baltimore: Ottenheimer Publishers, 1963.

Ames, L., & Ilg, F. Sex differences in test performance of matched girl-boy pairs in the five-to-nine-year-old range. *Journal of Genetic Psychology,* 1964, 104, 25-34.

Anastasiow, N. J. Success in school and boys' sex-role patterns. *Child Development,* 1965, 36, 1053-1066.

Ausubel, D. P. *Theory and problems of adolescent development.* New York: Grune, 1954.

Ausubel, D. P. *Theory and problems of child development.* New York: Grune, 1957.

Bandura, A. Vicarious and self-reinforcement processes. In R. Glaser (Ed.), *The nature of reinforcement: A symposium of the Learning Research and Development Center, University of Pittsburgh.* New York: Academic Press, 1971.

Bandura, A., & Huston, A. C. Identification as a process of incidental learning. *Journal of Abnormal and Social Psychology,* 1961, 63, 311-318.

Bandura, A., & Perloff, B. Relative efficacy of self-monitored and externally imposed reinforcement systems. *Journal of Personality and Social Psychology*, 1967, 7, 111-116.

Barrett, R. L. Changes in accuracy of self-estimates. *Personnel and Guidance Journal*, 1968, 47, 353-357.

Biller, H. B. Father absence, maternal encouragement, and sex role development in kindergarten-age boys. *Child Development*, 1969, 40, 539-546.

Biller, H. B. Father absence and the personality development of the male child. *Developmental Psychology*, 1970, 2, 181-201.

Binder, D. M., Jones, J. G., & Strowig, R. W. Non-intellective self-report variables as predictors of scholastic achievement. *Journal of Educational Research*, 1970, 63, 364-366.

Boshier, R. Self esteem and first names in children. *Psychological Reports*, 1968, 22, 762.

Brookover, W. B., Thomas, S., & Paterson, A. Self-concept of ability and school achievement. *Sociology of Education*, 1964, 37, 271-278.

Brown, J. A. C. *Freud and the Post-Freudians.* Baltimore: Penguin, 1961.

Caplin, M. D. The relationship between self-concept and academic achievement. *Journal of Experimental Education*, 1969, 37, 13-16.

Carlson, R. Stability and change in the adolescent's self-image. *Child Development*, 1965, 36, 659-666.

Caskey, S. R., & Felker, D. W. Social stereotyping of female body image by elementary school age girls. *Research Quarterly*, 1971, 42, 251-255.

Clayson, M. D. Concept modification in institutionalized delinquents. *American Journal of Orthopsychiatry*, 1969, 39, 459-465.

Coons, W. H., & McEachern, D. L. Verbal conditioning, acceptance of self and acceptance of others. *Psychological Reports*, 1967, 20, 715-722.

Coopersmith, S. A method for determining types of self-esteem. *Journal of Abnormal and Social Psychology*, 1959, 59, 87-94.

Cowen, E. L., Zax, M., Klein, R., Izzo, L. D., & Trost, M. A. The relation of anxiety in school children to school record, achievement, and behavioral measures. *Child Development*, 1965, 36, 685-695.

Craig, H. A sociometric investigation of the self-concept of the deaf child. *American Annals of the Deaf*, 1965, 110, 456-478.

Crandall, V. C., Katkovsky, W., & Crandall, V. J. Children's beliefs in their own control of reinforcements in intellectual-academic achievement situations. *Child Development*, 1965, 36, 91-109.

Diggory, J. C. *Self-evaluation: Concepts and studies.* New York: Wiley, 1966.

Dissinger, J. *Locus of control in achievement: Measurement and empirical assessment.* (Doctoral dissertation, Purdue University) Ann Arbor, Mich.: University Microfilms, 1968, No. 69-7437.

Dunn, J. A. The approach-avoidance paradigm as a model for the analysis of school anxiety. *Journal of Educational Psychology,* 1968, 59, 388-394.

Durrett, M. E. Relation between anxiety and self-concept among Marathi-speaking Indian children. *Journal of Home Economics,* 1965, 57, 717-719.

Epstein, S. The self-concept revisited: On a theory of a theory. *American Psychologist,* 1973, 28, 404-416.

Erikson, E. H. *Childhood and society.* (2nd ed.) New York: Norton, 1963.

Fagot, B. I., & Patterson, G. R. An in vivo analysis of reinforcing contingencies for sex-role behaviors in the preschool child. *Developmental Psychology,* 1969, 1, 563-568.

Felker, D. W. Relationship between self-concept, body build and perception of father's interest in sports in boys. *Research Quarterly,* 1968, 39, 513-517.

Felker, D. W. The relationship between anxiety, self-ratings, and ratings by others in fifth-grade children. *Journal of Genetic Psychology,* 1969, 115, 81-86.

Felker, D. W. Self-concept and self-administered verbal rewards. Proposal, May, 1970, Purdue University, Grant I-RO1-MH-19384, National Institute of Mental Health.

Felker, D. W. Prediction of specific self-evaluations from performance and personality measures. *Psychological Reports,* 1972, 31, 823-826.

Felker, D. W. Self-concept and self-administered verbal rewards. Progress Report, February, 1972, Purdue University, Grant RO1-MH-19384-02, National Institute of Mental Health.

Felker, D. W. Skinnerism and philosophy of education. *Proceedings of the 1972 annual meeting of the Ohio Valley Philosophy of Education Society.* Terre Haute: Indiana State University, 1973.

Felker, D. W., & Kay, R. S. Self-concept, sports interests, sports participation, and body type of seventh- and eighth-grade boys. *Journal of Psychology,* 1971, 78, 223-228.

Felker, D. W., & Milhollan, F. Acquisition of cognitive responses under different patterns of verbal rewards. *Journal of Genetic Psychology,* 1970, 116, 113-123.

Felker, D. W., & Stanwyck, D. J. General self-concept and specific self-evaluations after an academic task. *Psychological Reports,* 1971, 29, 60-62.

Felker, D. W., & Stanwyck, D. J. Should adults teach children to praise themselves? *Elementary School Guidance and Counseling,* 1973, 7, 178-181.

Felker, D. W., Stanwyck, D. J., & Kay, R. S. The effects of a teacher program in self-concept enhancement on pupils' self-concept, anxiety, and intellectual achievement responsibility. *Journal of Educational Research,* 1973, 66, 443-445.

Felker, D. W., & Thomas, S. B. Self-initiated verbal reinforcement and positive self-concept. *Child Development,* 1971, 42, 1285-1287.

Felker, D. W., & Treffinger, D. J. Self-concept, divergent thinking abilities, and attitudes about creativity and problem solving. A paper presented at the annual meeting of the American Educational Research Association, New York, 1971.

Festinger, L. *A theory of cognitive dissonance.* Stanford: Stanford University Press, 1957.

Fink, M. Self-concept as it relates to academic underachievement. *California Journal of Educational Research,* 1962, 13, 57-62.

Flanders, N. A., Morrison, B. M., & Brode, E. L. Changes in pupil attitudes during the school year. *Journal of Educational Psychology,* 1968, 59, 334-338.

Freud, S. *The collected papers of . . . .* In P. Rieff (Ed.), New York: Collier Books, 1963. 10 vols.

Fromm, E. *The art of loving.* New York: Harper, 1956.

Gergen, K. J. *The concept of self.* New York: Holt, 1971.

Ginott, H. G. *Between parent and child.* New York: Macmillan, 1965.

Glasser, W. in *Reality of success.* A film produced by Dave Bell Associates, distributed by Media Five, Hollywood, 1972.

Gorlow, L., Butler, A., & Guthrie, G. M. Correlates of self-attitudes of retardates. *American Journal of Mental Deficiency,* 1963, 67, 549-555.

Hall, C. S. *A primer of Freudian psychology.* New York: World, 1954.

Hebert, D. J. Reading comprehension as a function of self-concept. *Perceptual and Motor Skills,* 1968, 27, 78.

Heilbrun, A. B., Jr. An empirical test of the modeling theory of sex-role learning. *Child Development,* 1965, 36, 789-799.

Hetherington, E. M. Effects of paternal absence on sex-typed behaviors in Negro and white preadolescent males. *Journal of Personality and Social Psychology,* 1966, 4, 87-91.

Hoffer, E. *The true believer; Thoughts on the nature of mass movements.* New York: Harper, 1951.

Holmes, D. J. *The adolescent in psychotherapy.* Boston: Little, Brown, 1964.

Horowitz, F. D. Social reinforcement effects on child behavior. In W. W. Hartup & N. L. Smothergill (Eds.), *The young child: Reviews of research.* Washington, D.C.: National Association for the Education of Young Children, 1967.

James, W. *Principles of psychology.* New York: Holt, 1890. 2 Vols.

Jersild, A. T. *In search of self.* New York: Columbia University, 1952.

Jersild, A. T. *The psychology of adolescence.* New York: Macmillan, 1957.

Jersild, A. T. *The psychology of adolescence.* (2nd ed.) New York: Macmillan, 1963.

Kagan, J. The concept of identification. *Psychological Review,* 1958, 65, 296-305.

Kay, R. S. *Self-concept and level of aspiration in third and fourth grade children.* (Doctoral dissertation, Purdue University) Ann Arbor, Mich.: University Microfilms, 1972, No. 73-6054.

Kay, R. S., Felker, D. W., & Varoz, R. O. Sports interests and abilities as contributors to self-concept in junior high school boys. *Research Quarterly,* 1972, 43, 208-215.

Kellogg, R. L. A direct approach to sex-role identification of school-related objects. *Psychological Reports,* 1969, 24, 839-841.

Kelly, G. A. *The psychology of personal constructs.* New York: Norton, 1955. 2 vols.

Kennedy, J. F. *Profiles in courage.* New York: Harper, 1956.

Kohlberg, L., Yeager, J., & Hjertholm, E. Private speech: Four studies and a review of theories. *Child Development,* 1968, 39, 691-736.

Lecky, P. *Self-consistency.* New York: Island Press, 1951.

Lefcourt, H. M. Belief in personal control: Research and implications. *Journal of Individual Psychology,* 1966, 22, 185-195.

Lekarczyk, D. T., & Hill, K. T. Self-esteem, test anxiety, stress, and verbal learning. *Developmental Psychology,* 1969, 1, 147-154.

Lewis, C. S. *Surprised by joy: The shape of my early life.* New York: Harcourt, Brace, 1955.

Lipsitt, L. P. A self-concept scale for children and its relationship to the Children's Form of the Manifest Anxiety Scale. *Child Development,* 1958, 29, 463-472.

Lowe, C. M. The self-concept: Fact or artifact? *Psychological Bulletin,* 1961, 58, 325-336.

Marston, A. R. Self-reinforcement: The relevance of a concept in analogue research to psychotherapy. *Psychotherapy: Theory, Research, and Practice,* 1965, 2, 1-5.

Maslow, A. H. *Motivation and personality.* New York: Harper, 1954.

Maw, W. H., & Maw, E. W. Self-concepts of high- and low-curiosity boys. *Child Development,* 1970, 41, 123-129.

McCandless, B. R. *Children: Behavior and development.* (2nd ed.) Chicago: Holt, 1967.

McCarthy, D. Language development in children. In L. Carmichael (Ed.), *Manual of child psychology,* (2nd ed.) New York: Wiley, 1954.

Meissner, A. L., & Thoreson, R. W. Relation of self-concept to impact and obviousness of disability among male and female adolescents. *Perceptual and Motor Skills,* 1967, 24, 1099-1105.

Messer, S. B. The relation of internal-external control to academic performance. *Child Development,* 1972, 43, 1456-1462.

Mitchell, J. V., Jr. Goal-setting behavior as a function of self-acceptance, over- and under-achievement, and related personality variables. *Journal of Educational Psychology,* 1959, 50, 93-104.

Moore, T. Difficulties of the ordinary child in adjusting to primary school. *Journal of Child Psychology and Psychiatry and Allied Discipline,* 1966, 7, 17-38.

Morse, W. C., & Wingo, G. M. *Psychology and teaching.* (3rd ed.) Glenview, Illinois: Scott, Foresman, 1969.

Piaget, J. *The language and thought of the child.* New York: Harcourt, Brace, 1926.

Piers, E. V., & Harris, D. B. Age and other correlates of self-concept in children. *Journal of Educational Psychology,* 1964, 55, 91-95.

Pilisuk, M. Anxiety, self-acceptance, and open-mindedness. *Journal of Clinical Psychology,* 1963, 19, 387-391.

Poteet, J. A. *Behavior modification: A practical guide for teachers.* Minneapolis: Burgess, 1973.

Powell, M., O'Connor, H. A., & Parsley, K. M., Jr. Further investigation of sex differences in achievement of under-, average-, and over-achieving students within five IQ groups in grades four through eight. *Journal of Educational Research,* 1964, 57, 268-269.

Purkey, W. W. *Self-concept and school achievement.* Englewood Cliffs, N.J.: Prentice-Hall, 1970.

Rhine, R. J., Hill, S. J., & Wandruff, S. E. Evaluative responses of preschool children. *Child Development,* 1967, 38, 1035-1042.

Richardson, S. A., & Emerson, P. Race and physical handicap in children's preference for other children. *Human Relations,* 1970, 23, 31-36.

Robeck, M. C. Effects of prolonged reading disability: A preliminary study. *Perceptual and Motor Skills*, 1964, 19, 7-12.

Rogers, C. R. *Client-centered therapy*. Boston: Houghton Mifflin, 1951.

Rogers, C. R. My philosophy of interpersonal relationships and how it grew. *Journal of Humanistic Psychology*, 1973, 13, 3-15.

Rosenberg, M. The association between self-esteem and anxiety. *Journal of Psychiatric Research*, 1963, 1, 135-152.

Roth, R. M., & Puri, P. Direction of aggression and the non-achievement syndrome. *Journal of Counseling Psychology*, 1967, 14, 277-281.

Rotter, J. B. *Social learning and clinical psychology*. New York: Prentice-Hall, 1954.

Rotter, J. B. Generalized expectancies for internal vs. external control of reinforcement. *Psychological Monographs*, 1966, 80. (Whole No. 609).

Santrock, J. W. Paternal absence, sex typing, and identification. *Developmental Psychology*, 1970, 2, 264-272.

Sarason, I. G., & Koenig, K. P. Relationships of test anxiety and hostility to description of self and parents. *Journal of Personality and Social Psychology*, 1965, 2, 617-621.

Schell, R. E., & Silber, J. W. Sex-role discrimination among young children. *Perceptual and Motor Skills*. 1968, 27, 379-389.

Schlick, M. *Problems of ethics*. New York: Prentice-Hall, 1939.

Sears, R. R. Relation of early socialization experiences to self-concepts and gender role in middle childhood. *Child Development*, 1970, 41, 267-289.

Shaw, M. C., & Alves, G. J. The self-concept of bright academic underachievers: II. *Personnel and Guidance Journal*, 1963, 42, 401-403.

Silcock, A. Sex role. *Australian Preschool Quarterly*, 1965, 6, 22-26.

Staffieri, J. R. A study of social stereotype of body image in children. *Journal of Personality and Social Psychology*, 1967, 7, 101-104.

Stanwyck, D. J. *Self-concept development: A longtitudinal study*. (Doctoral dissertation, Purdue University) Ann Arbor, Mich.: University Microfilms, 1972, No. 73-15872.

Stanwyck, D. J., & Felker, D. W. Intellectual achievement responsibility and anxiety as functions of self-concept of third- to sixth-grade boys and girls. A paper presented at the annual meeting of the American Educational Research Association, New York, 1971.

Stanwyck, D. J., & Felker, D. W. Measuring the self-concept: A factor analytic study. A paper presented at the annual meeting of the National Council on Measurement in Education, New York, 1971.

Stanwyck, D. J., Felker, D. W., & Van Mondfrans, A. P. An examination of the learning consequences of one kind of civil disobedience. *Educational Theory*, 1971, 21, 146-154.

Sullivan, H. S. *Conceptions of modern psychiatry.* Washington, D.C.: William Alanson White Psychiatric Foundation, 1947.

Summers, D. L., & Felker, D. W. Use of the It scale for children in assessing sex-role preference in preschool Negro children. *Developmental Psychology,* 1970, 2, 330-334.

Sutton-Smith, B., Rosenberg, B. G., & Landy, F. Father-absence effects in families of different sibling compositions. *Child Development,* 1963, 39, 1213-1221.

Vener, A. M., & Snyder, C. A. The preschool child's awareness and anticipation of adult sex-roles. *Sociometry: A Journal of Research in Social Psychology,* 1966, 29, 159-168.

Watson, D. Relationship between locus of control and anxiety. *Journal of Personality and Social Psychology,* 1967, 6, 91-92.

Wattenburg, W. W., & Clifford, C. Relation of self-concepts to beginning achievement in reading. *Child Development,* 1964, 35, 461-467.

Werblo, D., & Torrance, E. P. Experiences in historical research and changes in self-evaluations of gifted children. *Exceptional Children,* 1966, 33, 137-141.

White, R. W. Motivation reconsidered: The concept of competence. *Psychological Review,* 1959, 66, 297-333.

Williams, R. L., & Cole, S. Self-concept and school adjustment. *Personnel and Guidance Journal,* 1968, 46, 478-481.

Wylie, R. C. *The self-concept: A critical survey of pertinent research literature.* Lincoln: University of Nebraska Press, 1961.

Young, Leontine. *Life among the giants.* New York: McGraw, 1966.

Index